The Story of
Astronomy
and Space

Usborne Quicklinks

The Usborne Quicklinks Website is packed with thousands of links to all the best websites on the internet. The websites include video clips, sounds, games and animations that support and enhance the information in Usborne Internet-linked books. You can see stunning photographs of space, find out how to buy a telescope, learn all about how astronauts train, and much, much more.

To visit the recommended websites for this book, go to the Usborne Quicklinks Website at **www.usborne-quicklinks.com** and enter the keywords: **astronomy and space**.

When using the internet please follow the internet safety guidelines displayed on the Usborne Quicklinks Website. The recommended websites in Usborne Quicklinks are regularly reviewed and updated, but Usborne Publishing Ltd. is not responsible for the content or availability of any website other than its own. We recommend that children are supervised while using the internet.

This is the Eta Carinae Nebula – a nebula is a cloud of dust and gas in space where stars are born. The previous page shows another part of the nebula.

The Story of Astronomy and Space

Louie Stowell

Illustrated by Peter Allen

Designed by Samantha Barrett,
Anna Gould & Stephen Moncrieff

Edited by Jane Chisholm

Consultants: Stuart Atkinson,
Dr. Patricia Fara, University of Cambridge,
& William Whyatt

Contents

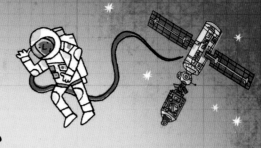

Chapter 1

Watching the skies

For thousands of years, people have looked up at the night sky and wondered what all those twinkling lights are trying to tell them. Long, long before a man walked on the Moon, even before someone realized that you could get a better look at the stars by putting glass lenses inside a long tube to make a telescope, human beings have studied the skies.

There were so many mysteries to solve. Where did the stars go during the day? Why did the Sun feel hotter in summer than in winter?

Modern scientists are still asking and answering new questions all the time, but there's still so much we don't know about outer space.

The Sun is yummy

In ancient China, people believed that an eclipse happened because a giant dragon was trying to eat the Sun.

They used to bang pots and pans and drums to frighten away the hungry monster. The Sun always came back, though, so they probably thought that it worked.

Thousands of years ago...

... a black circle slides across the face of the Sun. It's the middle of the day, but all becomes dark and cold. Mice and rabbits scurry to their burrows and the birds return to their nests, believing that night has come early.

Huddled together on the open plains, men and women cry out in fear at the unnatural darkness. What have they done to deserve this punishment from the gods? Has the Sun been snuffed out forever?

Today, we know that there is a far less scary explanation for the times when the Sun gets blotted out during the day. It's just the Moon passing in front of the Sun, blocking its light and causing what's known as a solar eclipse.

Although the Moon is a lot smaller than the Sun, it's also a lot closer to us. So, when the Moon passes between us and the Sun in its journey through the sky, it can cover the entire disc of the Sun, making it appear dark during the day.

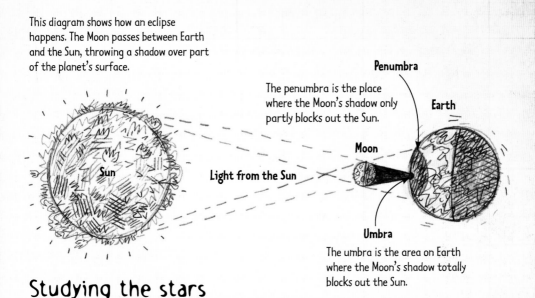

This diagram shows how an eclipse happens. The Moon passes between Earth and the Sun, throwing a shadow over part of the planet's surface.

Penumbra

The penumbra is the place where the Moon's shadow only partly blocks out the Sun.

Earth

Moon

Sun

Light from the Sun

Umbra

The umbra is the area on Earth where the Moon's shadow totally blocks out the Sun.

Studying the stars

All through human history, people have asked questions about what goes on among the stars. A lot of the answers have been wrong. But over time, curious, clever people have put together a better picture of how things fit together in the night sky.

We now know a lot about what's out there in space, thanks to a branch of science called astronomy. But there is still plenty left to discover.

What's astronomy?

Astronomy is the study of outer space and everything in it – the stars, the Moon, the planets, and more.

Astronomers investigate all the things you can see in the night sky, as well as things that are too far away for you to see. They're even interested in the ground under your feet, because they study the movement of Earth as it hurtles through space.

We three astronomers

The first astronomers were probably priests as well as stargazers.

Long ago, people believed that their gods ruled every part of their lives. Astronomers studied the skies to decide what the gods had in store.

The three wise men in the Bible may have been early astronomers.

Who does astronomy?

People who do astronomy as a paid job are professional scientists, and they often use very sophisticated equipment.

But a lot of important work is done by amateur astronomers, who are passionately interested in space and have learned a lot about it as their hobby – but they don't get paid to do it.

Some hard-working amateurs become very skilled, using sophisticated telescopes and other heavy-duty technology to study the skies.

You don't need fancy equipment to get involved in astronomy, though. Anyone who looks up at the sky and notices what's going on could be called an amateur astronomer. You could become one too.

All you need is a clear, dark night, and binoculars or a telescope if you want to get a closer look.

The professionals

There are lots of different types of professional astronomers, from astrophysicists (who do lots of tricky mathematics to do with space), to cosmologists (who study the way the Universe fits together), to planetary geologists. Planetary geologists study the landscapes of other planets, such as Mars, and try to discover what goes on under the surface there, as well as studying comets and other solid objects in space.

Robots on Mars

In 2003, a pair of remotely-controlled robots were sent to the surface of Mars. These machines – nicknamed "rovers" – were packed with gadgets so they could study the rocks and soil of the Martian landscape.

The rovers, named *Spirit* and *Opportunity*, have sent back tens of thousands of photos, giving us a close-up view of the surface of Mars.

Where do astronomers work?

Some astronomers even fly into space to do their experiments, but most are earthbound. They do their work using telescopes and laboratories, as well as sending up robots called space probes to beam back information from the distant corners of space.

Important amateurs

Both amateur and professional astronomers make important discoveries. In 1995, two men spotted a comet – a frozen bundle of ice, rocks and dust that shoots through space, trailing a glowing tail. Thomas Bopp, a keen amateur astronomer, was stargazing in Arizona when he saw the comet. The other comet spotter was a professional astronomer, Alan Hale.

Child astronomers

In 1930, a little girl named Venetia Burney and her grandfather were talking about a newly discovered planet that didn't have a name yet

Venetia thought it should be named Pluto, after a Roman god, since all the other planets were named after Roman gods.

Her grandfather passed the idea on to an astronomer he knew – and the name stuck.

Hale spotted the comet at home, from his driveway in New Mexico. The comet was named after both its discoverers – it's known as Comet Hale Bopp.

Comet Hale Bopp became visible to the naked eye in 1997, and it stayed visible for 18 months.

SILENCE

What's out in space?

There are all kinds of things out in the vast depths of space. From giant stars to tiny moons, from space dust to black holes, from planets made of gas to solid ones that people might live on one day.

When you first look up at the night sky, all the shining dots look more or less the same. But after a while you can see that some appear paler or brighter.

You'll see different shades too – red, blue or yellowish-orange. The longer you look, the more differences you'll spot.

In space, no one can hear you scream

In science fiction movies, you sometimes see two spaceships fighting. When one of them scores a deadly hit, you might hear a BOOM!

This would be impossible, in fact, as there's no sound in space, because there's no air to carry sound.

What can you see in the night sky?

Some of the bright dots in the sky are burning balls of gas called stars, that give off their own light. Other dots are planets, which don't make light of their own; they just reflect the Sun's light.

Every now and then, a comet will appear in the sky, such as Comet Hale Bopp. Some comets are too faint to see, but others are visible with the naked eye.

You might also see a streak of light that looks like a star falling through the sky. These "shooting stars" aren't stars at all. They're called meteors and they're caused by tiny pieces of dust and rock called meteoroids burning up in the blanket of gases – or atmosphere – that surrounds the Earth. Sometimes, parts of these rocks survive and land on Earth. These are known as meteorites.

Part of an astronomer's job is to predict when and where things like comets and meteors will appear in the sky. Often, whether you can see them will depend on where you live and how clear the skies are.

Rockets and planes

When you fly in a plane, you usually reach a height of about 10 km (6 miles) above the ground.

Some military planes go a lot higher, but not high enough to get into space. To do that, you need a rocket to blast you away from Earth.

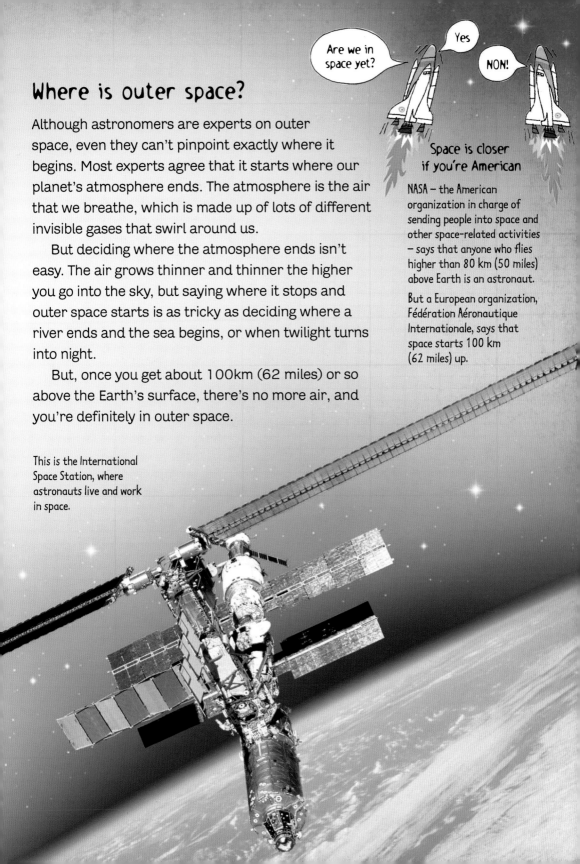

Where is outer space?

Although astronomers are experts on outer space, even they can't pinpoint exactly where it begins. Most experts agree that it starts where our planet's atmosphere ends. The atmosphere is the air that we breathe, which is made up of lots of different invisible gases that swirl around us.

But deciding where the atmosphere ends isn't easy. The air grows thinner and thinner the higher you go into the sky, but saying where it stops and outer space starts is as tricky as deciding where a river ends and the sea begins, or when twilight turns into night.

But, once you get about 100km (62 miles) or so above the Earth's surface, there's no more air, and you're definitely in outer space.

This is the International Space Station, where astronauts live and work in space.

Are we in space yet?

Yes

NON!

Space is closer if you're American

NASA – the American organization in charge of sending people into space and other space-related activities – says that anyone who flies higher than 80 km (50 miles) above Earth is an astronaut.

But a European organization, Fédération Aéronautique Internationale, says that space starts 100 km (62 miles) up.

What are light years?

Light years aren't years at all, but a way of measuring the massive distances in space without having to have numbers with lots and lots and lots of zeros.

One light year is the distance light travels in a year, which is a whopping 9.46 trillion km (5.9 trillion miles) – one trillion is a million times a million, or a one with twelve zeros.

How far to the nearest star?

One of the nearest stars to Earth is Proxima Centauri, about 4.2 light years away. Even the fastest spaceships would take over 100,000 years to arrive.

So, if astronauts flew there, only their distant descendants would actually arrive.

What is the Universe?

Astronomers study how the Universe fits together. The Universe is everything that exists and has ever existed and will ever exist. It's all the stars and planets and all the space in between them. That's a pretty big topic.

Mindbogglingly big questions

Astronomers ask big questions to match, such as, "Is there life on other planets?", "How did the Universe begin?" or, "Will Earth be destroyed by meteoroids?"

Space is full of gigantic objects, separated by enormous distances – distances you'd never have time to cross, even if you had the fastest possible spaceship, and if you lived for centuries.

As a science, astronomy is the opposite of looking at tiny things under a microscope, very close up. It's mostly about looking at massive things in the far, far, far distance.

Light from stars can travel for millions and millions of years before it reaches us. Planets travel fantastic distances at incredible speeds – the Earth itself is hurtling around the Sun at about 100,000 km/h (62,000 mph) – about 1,000 times faster than the top speed that even the craziest driver would hit on Earth.

Are we there yet?

This way to Proxima Centauri

It would take about a thousand times longer than a human lifespan to get to Proxima Centauri, one of our nearest stars.

You ask that every century!

14

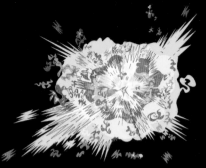

Looking into the past

Amazingly, some of the things that astronomers study – and that you can see in the night sky – don't exist any more. That's a baffling thing to get your head around, at first, but this is how it works...

Like everything in the Universe, stars die eventually – some even explode.

Now, the light from a star can take years to reach us across the vast distances of space. By the time it does, the star you think you're looking at might have exploded. It's a little like hearing an echo of someone shouting. Although they're not shouting any more, you can still hear it.

This means astronomers can literally look into the past and see how the Universe used to be. Studying the light from long-dead stars has helped scientists come up with theories about how the Universe began.

When stars go boom

When some very big stars get older, they end their lives with a massive, unimaginably violent explosion.

An exploding star is known as a supernova. Tiny particles of the dead star are hurled out into space in all directions.

This image – which was taken using a telescope out in space – shows the remnants of an exploding star, known as a supernova.

Magic or a trick?

A stage magician named The Amazing Randi once played a trick on a class of schoolkids.

He gave them all personal horoscopes. Most of the children said that theirs was true. But then, Randi revealed that all the horoscopes were identical.

The secret of his success was being vague. Horoscopes often use vague wording that could apply to almost anyone.

What about astrology?

Most magazines have horoscopes in them, telling people with a particular "star sign" what will happen to them in the week or month to come. Horoscopes are based on an ancient way of studying the skies called astrology.

Astrologers claim to predict your future by looking at how the planets and stars were lined up when you were born. There are different types of astrology, but the basic idea is that what happens in space affects the lives of each person on Earth.

Star signs are also known as signs of the zodiac. The dates of each sign vary depending on the year you're born.

Aquarius
January 20 – February 18

Pisces
February 19 – March 20

Aries
March 21 – April 19

Taurus
April 20 – May 20

Gemini
May 21 – June 20

Cancer
June 21 – July 22

Leo
July 23 – August 22

Virgo
August 23 – September 22

Libra
September 23 – October 22

Scorpio
October 23 – November 21

Sagittarius
November 22 – December 21

Capricorn
December 22 – January 19

Is it true?

Although reading your horoscope and being told that you're going to win loads of money, or travel the world, is fun, there is no evidence to prove that astrology works.

Astrologers talk about a mysterious "pull" that planets have on us, but it's not something that can be measured, and no one has explained satisfactorily how it works.

If astrology were true, people born at the same time in the same place would lead similar lives. But studies done on "astro twins" haven't shown this at all. Of course, horoscopes are often vague, so they can *seem* to come true if you want to believe in them.

The stars say Hitler will attack tomorrow!

Onomy and Ology

Astronomy and astrology were actually mixed together for a long time. In the past, many astronomers who made accurate observations of the skies also believed in the mystical power of the planets and other heavenly bodies.

An ancient people called the Babylonians, for example, could predict eclipses based on their observations. But they also believed that eclipses contained special messages about human destinies.

It was only during the 17th century that astronomy and astrology really started to go their separate ways. There was a big shift in the way humans understood the world at this time, and scholars started to focus more on physical things that you can measure. Mathematical astronomy grew more and more important, while astrology was pushed aside.

Nonsense and science

A few thousand years ago, stargazers in the ancient kingdom of Babylon made a lot of observations that we'd call "scientific" today.

But what they did with this information was often not scientific at all.

For example, Babylonian stargazers might correctly predict an eclipse – so far, so scientific – but then explain the eclipse as a good omen for the king.

This amazing light show
is known as the Northern
Lights or Aurora Borealis – its
scientific name in Latin. It's
caused by particles (a scientific
word for some of the smallest
things we know of) from the
Sun colliding with the Earth's
atmosphere.

Chapter 2

Great balls of fire and a little ball of rock

You can't see our nearest star anywhere in the night sky. It can only be seen during the day. That's because it's the Sun. Like all stars, our Sun is a gigantic ball of burning gas. Sounds dangerous?

It often is. Although the Sun's a long way away, too much sunlight can burn your skin and even give you cancer. But we also need the Sun to survive.

The Sun gives us energy. It governs the seasons, the harvests, and even our sleep patterns. No wonder the Sun god was the boss in many ancient religions.

The other stars are too far away for us to feel their heat. But many of them are just as powerful up close. Many are much hotter still. By comparison, the Moon doesn't seem very impressive. It's just a dead lump of rock that reflects the light of the Sun. But even the Moon has its own powers over Earth.

What is the Sun?

The Sun is a gigantic, unimaginably hot ball of burning gases. It's mostly made of hydrogen – which is found in all sorts of things, from water to fertilizer, to nuclear bombs – and helium – which is used in floating party balloons.

The Sun's gases don't burn like wood or coal, which need the oxygen in the air to set them alight. The Sun burns without any oxygen.

At its core, the gases are so dense that their atoms (tiny building blocks of the Universe) get smashed together. This creates explosions that produce the Sun's heat and light.

Don't look now... or at all, ever!

If you want to look at the Sun... don't! It can damage your eyes – and even make you blind if you look directly at its fiery face.

Astronomers have special equipment to look at it, but you can Sun-gaze safely with a home-made viewing device. (You need a pair of binoculars to make this.)

Put the caps on both ends of one side of a pair of binoculars. Prop up a piece of white cardboard and point one end of the binoculars at the Sun, and the other at the cardboard.

Look at the bright circle that will appear on the cardboard. Do NOT look through the binoculars. Twiddle the focus to get a sharp image.

Warning: don't get your sleeves or hands in the way of

Bright sparks

The Sun looks still and quiet in the sky, but in fact it's always churning and changing. Loops of burning gas, called prominences, whoosh up from the surface at up to 600 km (375 miles) per second. From time to time, massive explosions known as solar flares burst out too. Particles from these explosions zoom across space and hit Earth's atmosphere. This can sometimes mess with the equipment of airline pilots – luckily, though, not enough to make them crash. Major flares have the power to fry the workings of satellites, disrupt TV and radio signals and lead to

Our friendly local star

If the Sun was a lot farther away, it would look like the other stars: a twinkling point of light. But, because it's a lot closer than they are, it looks huge and feels hot. Even though it's not very hot as stars go, it's close enough for a lot of its heat to reach us. Still, even though it's close in star terms, the Sun is still about 150 million km (93 million miles) away from Earth.

Earth belongs to a set of planets and other objects that go around the Sun. Together, the Sun and its planets are known as the Solar System.

Compared to the Sun, the planets are tiny. The picture below shows Venus passing between Earth and the Sun. You can see just how tiny Venus is by comparison. It's roughly the same size as Earth.

How big? How hot?

● If the Sun were a hollow ball, you could fit about a million Earths inside it.

● If you flew in the direction of the Sun in a spaceship, your craft would burn up before you got within a few million miles.

● If the Sun was the size of a basketball, Earth would be the size of a pinhead.

● The Sun reaches up to 15 million °C (27 million °F) in its middle.

This photograph shows Venus passing between Earth and the Sun.

Venus

The spotted Sun

If you use the viewing device on page 20 to project an image of the Sun onto some cardboard, you might see dark blotches on the projected image.

These are sunspots – areas on the Sun's surface that are cooler than the rest, which makes them appear darker.

The surface of the Sun is always changing, so sunspots appear and disappear.

But they're not just little spots. They're usually about 20,000 km (12,000 miles) across.

...then there was one

In Ancient Chinese mythology, there were ten suns. They usually took turns in the sky, but one day they decided to appear all at once.

This made it unbearably hot so people asked them to take turns again.

When the suns refused, the god who was the father of all these naughty suns sent another god down from heaven to scold them. But he ended up destroying nine of the suns.

Legend has it that the one that was spared is the Sun we see today.

Inside the Sun

The Sun isn't the same all the way through. It has layers that are different temperatures. The middle is the hottest part and the surface is the coolest. Here's how they all fit together.

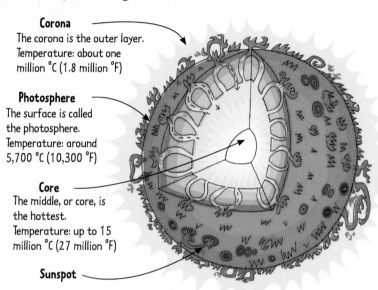

Corona
The corona is the outer layer.
Temperature: about one million °C (1.8 million °F)

Photosphere
The surface is called the photosphere.
Temperature: around 5,700 °C (10,300 °F)

Core
The middle, or core, is the hottest.
Temperature: up to 15 million °C (27 million °F)

Sunspot

Far bigger than the biggest planet

The Sun is so huge that if you put Earth and all the other planets in the Solar System on one side of a weighing scale, and the Sun on the other, the Sun would still be almost a hundred times heavier. The Sun makes up 99.8% of the Solar System's "mass" – a scientific term for how much stuff or "matter" there is in an object. Mass is a particularly useful idea when you're trying to understand how objects behave in outer space. When scientists talk about weight, they mean the mass of an object, multiplied by how much it's pulled by something called gravity...

And gravity is...?

Weeeeeeeeee!

Gravity is a force. The simplest way to describe a force is to say that it's a push or a pull. Gravity is a force that pulls objects together. All objects – from pencil sharpeners to planets – have a gravitational pull.

The strength of this pull depends on an object's mass. You can't feel the pull of small objects but the bigger something's mass, the stronger its pull.

Earth's mass is huge, which is why objects fall when you drop them. The Sun has an even more powerful pull. This is what stops Earth and the other planets from shooting off into space.

A weaker pull

The Moon's gravitational pull isn't as strong as the Earth's, because the Moon is smaller.

So, you'd weigh a lot less on the Moon than on Earth, even though the amount of stuff that makes up your body stays the same.

It's easier to talk about the mass of something than its weight, when you're talking about different places in space, because mass doesn't vary with gravity.

Spaceship Earth

The Earth travels around the Sun in a not-quite-circular motion, known as orbiting.

As Earth orbits the Sun, it spins around its own axis – an imaginary line through its middle – once every 24 hours. When one side of the planet faces the Sun, the other side is plunged into darkness. So, when it's daytime on one side, it's night on the other.

Although Earth is moving at 108,000 km/hr (67,000 mph), you can't feel it. This is because its speed stays the same.

If Earth sped up, you'd feel it – just as when the driver puts his or her foot down in a car.

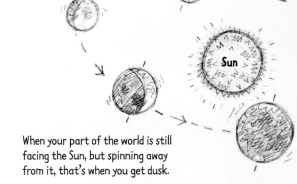

Sun

When your part of the world is still facing the Sun, but spinning away from it, that's when you get dusk.

Danger in the Sun

The Sun doesn't just provide us with bright sunshine. It also gives off light that the human eye can't detect.

One type of invisible light that it emits is called UV (ultraviolet) radiation. It can be harmful to humans if they get too much of it.

This is what makes you burn if you're outside too long when it's hot. It can also give you skin cancer.

Plants use the energy from the Sun to make food. This process is known as photosynthesis.

Just hot enough

If the Earth was much closer to or farther away from the Sun, we wouldn't be here. Just like Baby Bear's porridge in *Goldilocks and the Three Bears*, Earth was "just right" for life to develop – the range of temperatures here allowed plants and animals (including us) to thrive. If we were as close to the Sun as the planet Mercury, for example, it would've been far too hot for life as we know it to develop.

But it's not just about distance from the Sun. The gases in our atmosphere help protect us from some of the harmful rays the Sun sends our way, and they also help to keep the temperature steady.

What does the Sun do for us?

If the Sun was snuffed out tomorrow, we'd freeze to death pretty quickly. But even if we managed to keep warm somehow, the plants would die because they couldn't make food. Without plants, animals and humans would starve. We'd also suffocate, because plant life produces the oxygen we breathe.

Christmas on the beach

Picture the scene: it's Christmas Day and you're lying on the beach. If that sounds chilly, you probably live in one of the planet's northern countries, known as the northern hemisphere. But if you live in one of the southern countries, known as the southern hemisphere, it would be summer at Christmas time.

This is because the Earth orbits the Sun at an angle. Different parts of Earth are angled towards the Sun at different times of the year. When your hemisphere is tilted towards the Sun, it'll be summer, as the Sun's rays hit that part of the Earth more strongly.

The Equator

There's an imaginary line running around the middle of the Earth, where the northern and southern hemispheres meet.

This is the Equator, and it runs through countries such as Somalia and Brazil.

At the Equator, the Sun's rays always hit the Earth at the same angle – head on – so there isn't much variation in temperature.

The amount of rain does vary though, so you get a wet season and a dry season.

In March, neither hemisphere is warmed more, so it's spring in the north and autumn in the south.

In January, it's summer in the southern hemisphere.

In June, the northern hemisphere is enjoying its summer.

Again, in September, neither hemisphere gets warmed more.

A little experiment

Try shining a flashlight directly at the ground. The ground should be lit up brightly. This is how the Sun shines in summer.

Now, try shining the flashlight at an angle. The light will spread out more and look paler. This is how the Sun shines in winter – the light is more spread out so it's colder.

During the summer, the days are longer and the nights are shorter. If the Earth didn't tilt, day and night would be the same length all year round.

Our faithful companion

A chip off the old block?

No one knows for sure how the Moon came into existence.

One likely theory says that a huge rock the size of the planet Mars bashed into the Earth about four billion years ago, sending a cloud of debris flying out into space.

This debris got trapped in orbit by the Earth's gravity, forming a ring. Over time, these pieces grouped into a ball – the Moon.

One day, we'll be the Moon!

Dark or far side?

We only ever see one side of the Moon. The side that's hidden from us is often called the "dark side" – although it's really the "far side" – as it isn't actually dark all the time.

It faces the Sun just as often as the rest of the Moon does.

But it always faces away from Earth, because of the way the Moon rotates as it orbits us.

The Moon is a big ball of rock that orbits Earth, just as we orbit the Sun. But while Earth and the Sun are changing all the time, the Moon stays pretty much the same. It's just a big ball of rock.

That may sound dull, but when you're looking at it from Earth, it's the second brightest object in the sky, after the Sun. It's close enough that you can see a lot of its craters, mountains, and other interesting lumps and bumps, with binoculars or a small telescope.

Unlike the Sun, the Moon doesn't give off its own light, so it's perfectly safe to stare at it. On a clear night, it can be a beautiful sight. It's been a popular topic for love songs and poems throughout history, and some people have even believed that the Moon has magic powers – that it could drive people insane, or turn them into wolves.

I'll get you one day!

Tugging at the oceans

The Moon can't turn people into wolves, but it does have the power to move oceans. Whenever the sea creeps away from the beach at low tide or sneaks back up at high tide, the Moon is responsible.

As the Moon's gravity pulls at the Earth, the planet's surface bulges out on both sides – the side nearest the Moon, and at the spot directly opposite it.

You can't tell when the land is bulging out, since solid rock doesn't get pulled as much as liquid, but the effect on the sea is dramatic.

The bulging of the water causes tides, which are basically a wave that moves at a snail's pace through the sea. When the highest part of the wave reaches a particular coastline, it's called a high tide. When the wave has moved far away, you get a low tide.

As the Earth spins on its axis, different parts of the oceans are pulled at by the Moon. Each coastline gets two high and two low tides every 24 hours.

Tides are also affected by the pull of the Sun's gravity. But, because the sun is a lot farther away, it has much less impact, even though it's much bigger.

Starving Moon

An Inuit legend says that the Moon is a god called Anningan, who spends his life chasing the Sun goddess through the sky.

Sometimes he gets so caught up in the chase that he forgets to eat, getting thinner until he becomes a skinny crescent.

Eventually he remembers to eat and fattens up into a Full Moon again, and the chase continues.

It's just a phase

Each night, the Moon shows us a slightly different face – from a round Full Moon to a skinny Crescent Moon. These shifting shapes are known as phases.

The Moon doesn't literally change shape. It just looks as if it does because the Sun's rays light up different areas of the Moon as it orbits us. We see more or less of its face depending on where it is in relation to the Sun, and how much light is falling on it.

Waxing Crescent Moon

First Quarter

Full Moon

Last Quarter

Waning Crescent Moon

27

Star bears and sky hunters

Astronomers divide the night sky into 88 areas, known as constellations. You will see different ones depending on which hemisphere you live in, and on the time of year. Most constellations are named after animals, objects or people, although they often don't look much like the thing they're named after.

Orion and Ursa Major are a couple of the most famous ones. Orion is named after a hunter from an ancient Greek myth. Ursa Major is supposed to look like a bear and its name means "Big Bear" in Latin. But if you draw lines between the stars on a map of the constellations, you get a weirdly shaped hunter and a funny looking bear.

Different cultures have seen different pictures in the sky. The constellation Scorpius, for example, got its name from a Greek myth about a scorpion. But, in ancient China, the same stars were part of a dragon-shaped constellation. And in Hawaii, the tail of Scorpius is known as Maui's Fishhook, after a god who pulled the Hawaiian Islands up from the sea. But the Greek and Roman names are the ones that stuck.

Turn left at Betelgeuse

There's nothing scientific about the way that stars are grouped into constellations and the stars in them aren't necessarily close together. But constellations are still useful. On a clear night, you might see thousands of stars, so it helps to have an easy way to find your way around the sky. If you can spot, say, Orion, that'll help you spot a star named Betelgeuse. This enormous star marks the "shoulder" of Orion.

Here are some of the most famous constellations.

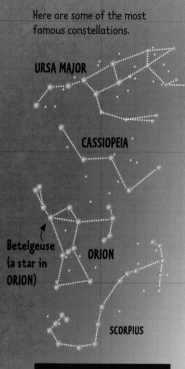

URSA MAJOR

CASSIOPEIA

Betelgeuse (a star in ORION)

ORION

SCORPIUS

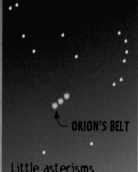

ORION'S BELT

Little asterisms

You can also look for smaller groups, known as asterisms. These are made up of parts of constellations, or from stars in different constellations. For example, three bright stars at the middle of Orion make up an asterism named Orion's Belt.

This picture shows a galaxy known as NGC 1300. This shape of galaxy is known as a barred spiral galaxy.

The Milky Way and other galaxies

All the stars you can see in the night sky without a powerful telescope are part of a group – or galaxy – named the Milky Way. We're actually inside the Milky Way – which is also known as "the Galaxy" with a capital "G" at the start.

With the naked eye, you can see some other bright galaxies as smears or clouds of light, but you can't make out individual stars. Other galaxies can only be seen using powerful telescopes.

So far, astronomers have spotted some that are up to 15 billion light years away. There are millions and millions of galaxies in the Universe, each with billions of stars in them.

Too close for photos

Spaceships can't get far enough away to take a photo of the Galaxy from the outside.

But scientists have pieced together what it probably looks like by studying its stars and the way other galaxies behave. It's probably a spiral shape, a little like the galaxy in the picture above.

Galactic slow dance

Galaxies are constantly rotating, on a slow spin cycle that takes millions of years.

Our Galaxy takes 230 million years to rotate once – measured as the time it takes the Sun to orbit the Galaxy's middle. This is also known as a galactic year. It's just one of these years since dinosaurs walked the Earth.

The two galaxies in this picture are colliding – ever so slowly.

Astronomers predict that NGC 2207, the larger galaxy on the left, will eventually swallow IC 2163, the smaller galaxy on the right, forming one huge galaxy.

In a galaxy far, far ago

The light from stars takes years to reach us, so we're looking back in time when we stargaze. But how far back are we talking about?

The farthest stars in our own Galaxy are 100,000 light years away, so light from those stars would've started its journey long before history began. The light from other galaxies has even farther to travel.

A galaxy that's sometimes visible with the naked eye, called the Andromeda galaxy, is 2½ million light years away. When its light reaches your eyes, you're seeing it as it was 2½ million years ago.

The lives of stars

All sorts of things could happen to a star in the time it takes for its light to reach us. Stars live busy lives: they burn, move, grow – even explode. Usually, the bigger the star, the bigger the drama.

Sometimes, the galaxy that a star "lives" in collides with another. This isn't like two cars crashing – it's more like two clouds merging, forming spectacular new shapes.

From little clumps to dying giants

All stars begin their lives in vast clouds of gas and dust, called nebulae. As these clouds swirl around in space, clumpy bits form inside them. When a clump grows into a giant ball, explosive reactions begin at the hot, dense core. The ball starts to burn fiercely, and a star is born.

Eventually, all stars run out of fuel and cool down, but this tends to take a very long time. Our Sun, for example, has about four billion* years of fuel left.

Most stars expand and turn red as they cool, becoming objects known as red giants. After that, stars of about our Sun's size shrink into a "white dwarf" – about the size of a planet, but an awful lot denser. Imagine a golf ball that weighs the same as a truck. But it's a peaceful end. White dwarves cool and die quietly.

Bigger stars – more than 1 ½ times the Sun's mass – make a more dramatic exit, exploding as a spectacular supernova.

*A billion is a thousand times a million or one with nine zeros.

The Orion Nebula is so bright that it's visible to the naked eye. About 700 stars have been observed forming there.

Live fast, die pretty

Some scientists think that when Eta Carinae, one of the brightest stars in our Galaxy, explodes, it'll be so bright that you could read by its light at night.

It's hard to predict when it will explode, though. It could be in 10,000 years – or it could be tomorrow.

Hurry up and die – I want to read!

Chapter 3

Wanderers in space

As we circle the Sun, we've got company. Earth is just one of many objects in orbit around the Sun – the star at the heart of our Solar System.

The largest of these circling objects are the planets, although there are plenty of others, from chunks of rock and ice to grains of dust.

If you glance up at the sky, the planets look a little like stars, but stars and planets are as different as fire and ice. And the planets themselves are a very varied bunch – from huge gas giants and tiny Moon-like balls of rock, to the warm, wet planet that we call home.

This photo of Mars shows its reddish-orange surface. But even when it's just a tiny dot in the sky, Mars has a reddish tinge.

Pesky things won't stay still!

What is a planet?

Planets are basically huge objects in orbit around a star. In our Solar System, that means the Sun. Every planet's orbit is a different size, which means that a year is a different length on each one – because a year is counted as roughly one orbit of the Sun.

The planets nearest the Sun – Mercury, Venus, Earth, then Mars – are known as the inner planets. They're smallish and rocky, and you could stand on the solid surface of any of them, although you'd boil, freeze or choke on all of them except Earth.

The outer planets – Jupiter, Saturn, Uranus, then Neptune – are much larger. They're made out of ice, gas and sloppy liquids, so you'd sink into them if you tried to land. Some planets have their own moons, and astronomers are still discovering new moons around faraway planets.

Wandering stars

The word "planet" comes from an ancient Greek word meaning "wanderer" – Greek astronomers observed that, while the stars kept in the same positions in relation to each other, the planets seemed to wander around in the sky.

Lonely Earthlings

There are no little green men on Mars. Scientists haven't even found little green patches of moss.

Earth is the only place where life definitely exists. But we might still find life on Mars one day, or on Europa, one of Jupiter's moons, or on planets orbiting other stars.

This diagram of the Solar System is not to scale. The Sun is so enormous, and the distances are so vast, that it wouldn't all fit on the same page if you did draw it to scale.

To be or not to be?

Maybe not?

Saturn

Jupiter

Discovering and losing planets

Astronomers have known about five of the planets (not counting Earth) since ancient times. Those five planets – Mercury, Venus, Mars, Jupiter and Saturn – are known as the "naked eye" planets, because they're "bright" enough to see with the naked eye. But planets don't give off light; they just reflect the Sun's glow.

It wasn't until 1690, after the telescope was invented, that someone spotted Uranus – though it was thought to be a star until 1781. Neptune was discovered in 1846, and, finally, Pluto in 1930.

Or not so finally, as it turned out. Fast forward to 2003, when some new, planet-like objects of about Pluto's size were discovered. This made Pluto's status a little muddy. So, in 2006, a group of astronomers came up with the first official definition of a planet. This was bad news for Pluto – it was reclassified a "dwarf planet" because it didn't make the grade.

Planet update

According to the International Astronomical Union (a group of important astronomers) a planet is:

• in orbit around the Sun.

• round (or more or less round).

• big enough to clear the area around it. That means it either pulls any surrounding rocks and debris down to its surface, or it pulls them into orbit around it.

There are also some dwarf planets, including Pluto. But not all astronomers agree with the definition above, and Pluto may one day be considered a planet again.

Mercury

Pluto
(Not currently
a planet)

Uranus

Mars

Venus

Sun

Moon

Earth

Neptune

Named after: the Roman messenger god

Diameter: about 4,880 km (3,032 miles)

Distance from Sun: varies a lot, from about 70 million km (43.5 million miles) to 46 million km (28.5 million miles)

Length of year: 88 Earth days

Length of day: 59 Earth days

Temperature: -170 °C to 427 °C (-275 °F to 800 °F)

Atmosphere: Very thin

Moons: None

Weather: Not much, due to the lack of atmosphere

Scientists have learned a lot about the planets in our Solar System by using powerful telescopes. They've also sent robot spacecraft known as probes to orbit them all and send back pictures and information. But, so far, probes have only actually landed on Mars and Venus.

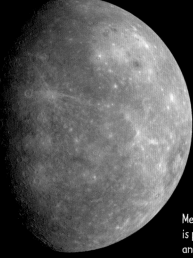

Mercury's surface is pock-marked and rocky, like the surface of the Moon.

A shrinking planet?

Some scientists think that Mercury may be shrinking. The theory is that, as the planet's molten core cools, it's getting smaller. Most things contract, or get smaller, as they cool.

Some scientists say the planet has shrunk by about 3 km (2 miles) over time.

The speedy one: Mercury

Tiny little Mercury is named after a Roman messenger god, who zipped through the sky on winged sandals. The planet lives up to its name – it only takes 88 Earth days to orbit the Sun. But it rotates so slowly that a day on Mercury is the same as 59 Earth days.

You wouldn't be able to breathe there, as there's hardly any atmosphere. You'd also bake or freeze, depending on when you visited. In the day, it's hot enough to melt lead, but during the long nights, the temperature plummets as low as -170 °C (-275 °F).

The poisonous one: Venus

Venus has plenty of gas around it to keep the heat in. Too much for comfort, since the thick atmosphere traps the Sun's rays like the glass of a greenhouse. This is known as a greenhouse effect. As a result, Venus is the hottest planet in the Solar System.

The surface of Venus is completely hidden by thick, fast-moving, poisonous clouds. These clouds would melt your spacesuit and eat into your flesh if you went there. You wouldn't be able to breathe anyway, as the "air" is mostly made up of carbon dioxide – the gas that humans breathe out. And, to add to the list of reasons not to visit Venus, the atmosphere is so heavy that the air pressure would crush you.

Venus fact file:

Named after: the Roman goddess of love

Diameter: about 12,100 km (7,520 miles)

Avg. dist. from Sun: 108.2 million km (67.2 million miles)

Length of year: 225 Earth days

Length of day: 243 Earth days

Average temp.: 465 °C (870 °F)

Atmosphere: Very thick, mostly carbon dioxide, with acid clouds

Moons: None

Weather: Storms above the surface, with high-speed winds

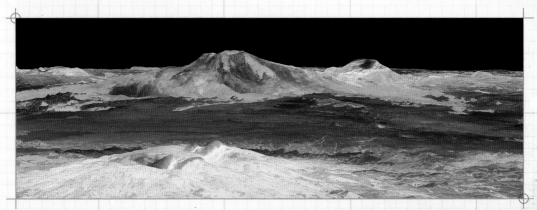

Voyage to Venus

The hidden surface of Venus was a mystery for ages. Scientists thought it might be a huge swamp, or even a tropical paradise. But, since the 1960s, various probes have visited Venus, and we now have maps of most of its surface. But, craft have only ever been able to survive briefly on the surface, before their instruments were wrecked by the scorching heat and pressure.

This computer-generated view of the surface of Venus was created using information sent back by the *Magellan* probe.

Venus used to be called Earth's twin planet. It's just a little smaller, but has similar landscape features, such as volcanoes.

Best beaches in the Solar System

Earth is the best place to hit the beach – the only place, if you like swimming. It's the only planet with liquid water that you can swim in.

Jupiter's moon Europa has lakes of liquid water, but they're frozen over. Saturn's moon Titan has lakes of liquid methane, but they're freezing – and poisonous too.

Very strange aliens?

All living things that we know of have carbon in them, so scientists tend to assume that life in other parts of the Universe will also be carbon-based (if we ever find any).

But it may be possible for life to form that's not carbon-based.

I'm carbon free!

The sopping wet one: Earth

We live on a sopping wet sponge of a planet. Over 70% of the Earth's surface is covered in oceans, streams, lakes and rivers. Perhaps we should we rename it "Water"?

Then again, it's also a rocky planet. Beneath the oceans and where the land is, there's a layer of solid rock, known as the crust. Under that are layers of solid rock, hot liquid rock, hot liquid metal and hot solid metal.

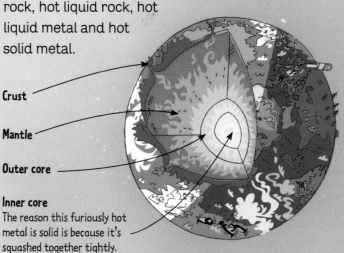

Crust

Mantle

Outer core

Inner core
The reason this furiously hot metal is solid is because it's squashed together tightly.

The ingredients of life

One of the reasons we have lots of liquid water is because the temperature on Earth is between the freezing and boiling points of water. That's thanks to our just-right distance from the Sun, and the fact that the gases in our atmosphere protect us from the extremes of heat and cold out in space.

One of these gases is the oxygen that we breathe. But our planet provides lots of other ingredients that make life possible, such as a substance called carbon. After water, it's the stuff that we have most of in our bodies.

This photo of Earth
was taken by astronauts
orbiting the Moon.

Danger, humans!

Although Earth is an ideal home for humans, the way we're treating our planet is making it less hospitable. For example, burning coal and oil for fuel creates gases known as greenhouse gases. Having too much of these creates a greenhouse effect, where the heat is trapped inside the blanket of gases. Earth is getting warmer as a result, which could make some places uninhabitable in the future. Still, the greenhouse effect is unlikely to become as fierce as it is on Venus.

Outside, looking in

Although we live on Earth and can observe it as closely as we like, we've learned all kinds of new things about it by studying it from space.

For example, weather forecasters use data collected by spacecraft that orbit Earth, known as satellites, to predict the weather. Satellites also study parts of Earth that are hard to see, such as the beds of deep oceans.

Climate change

As the world gets warmer, the ice at the North and South Poles is melting. This is making sea levels rise, which is very worrying for people who live on low-lying islands and/or near coasts.

One day, some of those places will be under water.

Mars fact file:

Named after: the Roman god of war

Diameter: about 6,780 km (4212 miles)

Average distance from the Sun: 228,000,000 km (141,672,588 miles)

Length of a year: 687 Earth days

Length of a day: About 40 minutes longer than a day on Earth

Average temperature: -23 °C (-9.4 °F)

Atmosphere: Mostly carbon dioxide and very thin – 100 times thinner than Earth's

Moons: Two little ones: Deimos and Phobos

Weather: Dust storms can sometimes cloud the sky for weeks or even months.

The red one: Mars

When you look at Mars in the night sky, it has an orange-red tinge, because the soil on Mars is a rusty red. If you landed on the planet, you'd see a dusty landscape of red sand dunes and rocks spreading out before you. The soil looks red because it contains a lot of rusted iron. Many scientists think there used to be a lot of water on Mars, long ago, and the water is what made the iron rust.

Mars doesn't have any lakes or rivers on its surface now. But, in 2008, NASA's *Phoenix Lander* spacecraft did an experiment, which showed that there's still some frozen water there. By melting icy soil in one of its instruments, the robotic craft proved that there is frozen water lurking below the planet's chilly soil.

We've learned most of what we know about Mars from the spacecraft we've sent there. No humans have visited yet, but craft that have landed on the surface have sent back incredibly detailed pictures and done experiments that've taught us a lot about what it's like on – and under – the planet's surface.

This photo of the surface of Mars was taken by the *Spirit* rover.

Is there life on Mars?

There are no aliens walking or slithering around on Mars, and no evidence of life of any kind. But scientists might still find tiny life forms one day, as robot ships land in different spots and sift through the soil.

Mars may have had a thicker atmosphere once. That means it could've been warmer and had liquid water, making it more hospitable for life to develop.

The Asteroid Belt

Beyond Mars lies the Asteroid Belt, where thousands of chunks of rock, or rock and metal, orbit the Sun. These chunks are known as asteroids. They can be as small as a pebble, or hundreds of miles across.

Most of them stay in the Asteroid Belt, but some do cross Earth's orbit. If a large one crashed into us, it could spell disaster. It's unlikely to happen in the near future, but there are scientists who monitor asteroid movements just in case. Various anti-asteroid weapons have been suggested, such as nudging the asteroid off course using a spaceship.

Why does water matter?

Most of the water on Earth is found in our oceans. These vast areas of salty water are believed to be the birthplace of Earth's first life forms, around 3,500 million years ago.

Finding water on Mars – or on other planets or moons – means there's more of a chance that there could be life on the planet. Or, at least, there might have been once.

Did an asteroid kill the dinosaurs?

Very occasionally, asteroids smash into the Earth, leaving large craters, like the craters on the Moon. There's one in the sea near Mexico, where a massive asteroid is believed to have slammed into Earth 65 million years ago.

It would've caused more damage to Earth than thousands of nuclear bombs. It may even have been the reason that all the dinosaurs died out.

This is Jupiter with a couple of its many moons. The big spot on the surface is actually a giant storm. It's more than twice the size of Earth.

The great big one: Jupiter

Jupiter, Saturn, Uranus and Neptune are "gas giants" – they're made mostly of gas, but scientists think they may be liquid or even solid in the very middle.

Jupiter is the biggest planet in the Solar System by a long way. Our planet, for example, could fit inside it more than a thousand times over.

If Jupiter had been bigger still, it could even have become a star. That's because it contains lots of hydrogen, which is what stars use for fuel. If its mass had been 80 times greater, explosive reactions would have started inside it, turning it into a burning star.

Jupiter has gathered an impressive gang of moons around it, thanks to its super-strong gravity. 63 have been spotted so far, but there are probably more. Some of them are very lively – Io, for example, has lava flows that are thousands of miles long. There might even be life forms of some kind on the planet-sized Europa, down in the ocean under its icy crust.

Jupiter fact file:

Named after: the ruler of the Roman gods

Diameter: 142,984 km (88, 846 miles)

Av. dist. from Sun: 778.3 million km (484 million miles)

Length of year: 11.86 Earth years

Length of day: 9.9 Earth hours

Av. temp: -153 °C (-243 °F)

Atmos.: Hydrogen & helium

Moons: 63 and counting

Weather: Stormy and windy

The ringed one: Saturn

All the gas giants have rings around them, but Saturn's are the most impressive.

These rings are made mostly of ice chunks and a small amount of rock. These chunks can be as small as a fingernail, or as big as a car.

You can't see the rings around Saturn (or any of the gas giants) with the naked eye. So, although astronomers knew about Saturn in ancient times, no one saw the rings until after telescopes were invented.

Like Jupiter, Saturn has a lot of moons. One of them in particular, Titan, has caught the eye of scientists in search of alien life. It's bigger than Mercury and has a thick atmosphere with a lot of nitrogen. It's probably the only moon in the Solar System with an atmosphere of any kind. Although humans couldn't breathe there, and although it's so very cold, it's still possible that some bizarre form of life might exist.

Saturn fact file:

Named after: the Roman god of farming

Diameter: 120,536 km (74,897.5 miles)

Average distance from the Sun: Almost twice as far as Jupiter –1.4 billion km (886 million miles)

Length of a year: 29 Earth years

Length of a day: 10.5 Earth hours

Av. temperature: -178 °C (-288 °F)

Atmosphere: Similar to Jupiter

Moons: 60 known moons

Weather: Less stormy than Jupiter, but very fast winds and some intense storms

This picture of Saturn was taken using the Hubble Space Telescope.

Floating world

Saturn is massive, but it's the lightest planet, because its density – the amount of matter packed into the space it takes up – is so low. If there was an ocean big enough to fit Saturn in, it would float.

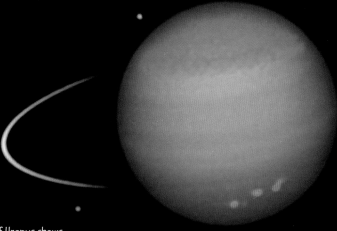

This image of Uranus shows its rings and six of its moons. A computer has been used to make the rings visible.

NOTE: when you say this planet's name, stress the first part, the "ur" part of the word.

Uranus fact file:

Named after: the Greek (and later, Roman) god of the skies

Diameter: 51,118 km (31,800 miles)

Average distance from the Sun: 3 billion km (1.8 billion miles)

Length of a year: 84 Earth years

Length of a day: 17.24 Earth hours

Av. temperature: -213 °C (-351 °F)

Atmosphere: Hydrogen, helium and a little methane

Moons: 27 known moons

Weather: Storms the size of the United States and steady temperatures

The wonky one: Uranus

It took a long time for astronomers to discover Uranus – or, at least, to recognize that it was a planet. An astronomer named John Flamsteed first spotted it in 1690, but he thought it was a star. Various astronomers saw it after that, and thought so too.

When a man named William Herschel first spied Uranus through his telescope in 1781, he thought it was a comet. People had believed for so long that there were only five planets that it didn't occur to him that there might be more. But as Herschel observed the bright object, he calculated that its orbit was wrong for a comet, and it was too far away. After comparing notes with other astronomers, he decided it was a planet.

Uranus is a gas giant, but both Uranus and Neptune are actually more icy than they are gassy. In fact, they're sometimes called the ice giants. Uranus is mostly rock and ice, with some gas.

What makes it stand out is that it orbits the Sun on its side. It may have been thrown into this strange spin after being smashed into by a large object long ago.

The far one: Neptune

After Uranus was discovered, astronomers noticed that something was pulling it out of its orbit. They decided that a large, unknown object must be affecting it.

Astronomers in France and Britain did calculations to predict where this object was and how big it would be. Using these predictions to guide him, a German astronomer named Johann Gottfried Galle spotted the planet in 1846.

Until a space probe flew there in 1989, Neptune seemed rather dull. But it actually has wild weather and the fastest winds in the Solar System. They reach up to 2000 km/h (1242 mph) – about the same speed as the fastest ever jet plane on Earth.

Neptune fact file:

Named after: the Roman god of the sea

Diameter: 49,528 km (30,775 miles)

Average distance from the Sun: 4.5 billion km (2.8 billion miles)

Length of a year: 164 Earth years

Length of a day: 16 Earth hours

Average temperature: -236 °C (-393 °F)

Atmosphere: Hydrogen, helium, water and methane – the methane makes it appear blue.

Moons: 13

Weather: The craziest weather in the Solar System with rapid winds, huge storms and quickly shifting clouds. Also has "spots" like Jupiter, which are actually storms.

The too-small one: Pluto

Pluto is a tiny, freezing, rocky little world. It's not just smaller than all the planets in the Solar System – it's even smaller than many of the moons. It's also very chilly and has a very thin atmosphere.

As it's so far away, no probes have been there yet, and it's hard to see it in much detail. Pictures taken using the most powerful telescopes suggest that Pluto may look like Neptune's moon, Triton, which is barren and rocky.

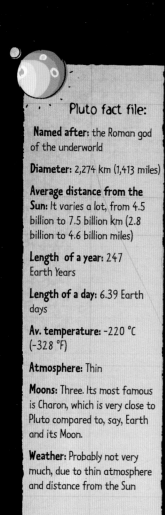

Pluto (on the left) and Charon, its closest moon

Trading places

No planet (or dwarf planet) has a perfectly circular orbit. Each one moves in an "ellipse" - a stretched-out circle or oval. Pluto's orbit is the most "eccentric" – that is, the most stretched out.

Its distance from the Sun varies so much that it's sometimes actually inside the orbit of Neptune. The next time this will happen will be in the year 2227.

Pluto was discovered after astronomers noticed that the orbits of Uranus and Neptune were being pulled out of shape by the gravity of an unknown object. "Must be a planet!" they thought, and the hunt for this orbit-bending "planet" began.

Pluto was spotted by American astronomer Clyde Tombaugh, in 1930, but it turned out to be too small to have much of a pull on Neptune and Uranus. Some astronomers decided there must be a "Planet X" tugging at them instead. But many astronomers now think that lots of little objects may be responsible

At the edge of the Solar System

YOU ARE NOW LEAVING SUN TOWN

After being demoted from planet to dwarf planet, Pluto got a consolation prize; in 2008, a new class of objects – the Plutoids – were named after it. Plutoids are large dwarf planets, and there are three of them so far, including Pluto itself.

The others are Eris – which is actually bigger than Pluto – Makemake (sounds like "macky macky") and Haumea. More Plutoids might join them, as there are a lot of large objects near Pluto. This part of space is known as the Kuiper Belt – it's basically a much colder version of the Asteroid Belt, full of icy, rocky objects.

Far beyond the Kuiper Belt lies an area that no one's ever seen. Astronomers think this is where some comets come from.

Comets can appear in the Solar System from any direction, so it's thought that there's a big cloud of them all around its edges. This is known as the Oort Cloud, after the Dutch astronomer Jan Oort, who came up with the idea in 1950.

Planets outside the Solar System

Lots of stars have planets orbiting them. These planets are known as extrasolar planets or exoplanets. The first exoplanet was discovered in 1991.

Over 300 others have been discovered so far. One day, we might find a rocky planet that has oceans, clouds and even life.

This comet is called Hyakutake. It was visible in 1996.

This is a sketch of the planet Saturn made during the 1700s by an English astronomer named Thomas Wright.

Chapter 4

Astronomy through the ages

Today, we know that the Earth goes around the Sun, and that stars are burning balls of gas. We know why the seasons happen, and that shooting stars aren't stars at all. But how did astronomers discover all those things – and more – in the first place?

It took thousands of years to build up the picture that we have today of how space works. Along the way, astronomers invented lots of clever tools to help them observe the skies. They also made plenty of mistakes and had a lot of furious arguments about what's true and what isn't.

This chapter explores some of the amazing discoveries – and crazy theories – that astronomers have made over the course of human history.

Astronomical circles

At Stonehenge, there is a pathway leading up to the main stone circle, known as the Avenue. Its direction lines up (more or less) with the Sun at the midsummer and the midwinter sunrise.

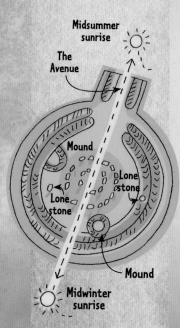

Outside the main circle are two mounds and two stones that form the corners of a rectangle.

The rectangle's sides line up with some of the Moon's movements.

So, the builders of Stonehenge may have used it to make observations of the Moon and the Sun.

Where did astronomy begin?

The first clues we have about early stargazers are mysterious stone circles, which are laid out so that some of their stones line up with sunrise and sunset at different times of year.

The most famous is Stonehenge, in south west England, which was begun around 5,000 years ago. It's hard to know for certain what it was used for, since it was built before the people who lived there started writing things down.

Some experts believe it may have been used to keep track of the seasons. Stonehenge and other stone circles were probably used as temples and burial grounds, too, and they may have been used in religious ceremonies.

This is a computer-generated image of Stonehenge. Archeologists use computer models such as this one to help them calculate the movements of the Sun, Moon and stars at Stonehenge.

What was astronomy for?

In ancient times, astronomy was vital for everyday life. The movements of the Sun, Moon, stars and planets were used to measure time and the seasons. Sailors and nomads – tribes of people who moved around a lot – used the stars to find their way.

Long ago, most people believed that everything that happened in the skies was caused by the gods – some thought that the planets and stars *were* gods. So stargazers looked for signs to tell them when to do important things, such as crowning a new king.

Pancake planet

Many early peoples believed that Earth was flat. They thought the sky must be a huge dome, with the stars, Sun and Moon attached to it.

No one ever went far enough to discover what happened when you reached the "edge" of the world.

The first written records

The first people to leave written records lived about 5,000 years ago in ancient Mesopotamia, where Iraq is now. In the years that followed, astronomers in that region made careful observations of what went on in the sky. They were also clever mathematicians, and we still use some of their ideas today, such as dividing an hour into sixty minutes.

Keeping tabs

Astronomers from an area in Mesopotamia, known as Sumer, kept detailed records of what they saw in the sky.

Some of their diaries still survive on clay tablets.

Seeing the future in the sky

Around 5,000 years ago in Egypt, astronomers (who were also priests) noticed that the star we now know as Sirius appeared and disappeared at the same times each year. Whenever it reappeared, the Nile river began to flood. This meant they were able to predict the floods – although they thought that it was the gods who caused them.

Ancient Chinese astronomers made careful observations and detailed maps of the stars but they also thought that the skies could tell them about the future. Chinese emperors employed astronomers to tell them what the stars foretold.

Each part of the sky was thought to mirror part of China. If a "bad omen" such as a comet appeared in a particular spot, the emperor might even attack the part of the country linked to that area of the sky.

Sky chariots

The ancient Egyptians thought that the Sun was a god, named Ra, who moved through the sky each day in a chariot.

They also believed that the Nile flooded each year because the goddess Isis was grieving for her dead husband, Osiris. Her tears filled up the river, making it overflow.

A clockwork computer

Thousands of years ago, an ingenious clockwork object, known as the Antikythera mechanism, was lost in a shipwreck.

When it was found by divers in 1901, it was badly rusted, but scientists pieced it together.

It's thought that the ancient Greek device once had moving parts that may have been used to keep track of the movements of the stars and planets.

Astronomy for its own sake

About 2,500 years ago, the ancient Greeks were the first people to do astronomy for its own sake, not just to "see" the future. Greek stargazers discovered how to measure the Earth, and found out how eclipses happen. By studying the movements of the planets, they learned to predict when they would appear.

The Greeks were the first to prove that the Earth is a globe. Before that, most people had thought it was flat. A man named Aristotle noticed how ships seem to vanish over the horizon. If the world was flat, he reasoned, they should just get smaller and smaller. Their sudden vanishing act only made sense if the Earth was curved.

In the middle of things

Most people in ancient times believed that Earth was in the middle of the Universe. They thought that the Sun and everything else circled around us – after all, the Sun does *seem* to travel across the sky each day.

But this left a puzzle for astronomers. Sometimes, the planets seemed to change direction and go back the way they'd come. A Greek astronomer named Ptolemy said it was because the planets were moving around in little circles as they circled the Earth.

Even though the planets don't actually circle the Earth, people were still able to predict the movements of the planets using Ptolemy's model. This was because it was based on careful observations of the patterns the planets made in the sky. Astronomers used his model for over a thousand years.

One Venus or two?

The ancient Greeks had two different names for the planet Venus.

At first, they thought it was two different objects, as Venus can appear in the morning or the evening, depending on the time of year.

But, later, about 2,500 years ago, the mathematician Pythagoras realized they were one and the same planet. He may have got this idea from a people called the Babylonians.

Ptolemy's model is known as a "geocentric" system. "Geo" means Earth in Greek, and geocentric means Earth is in the middle.

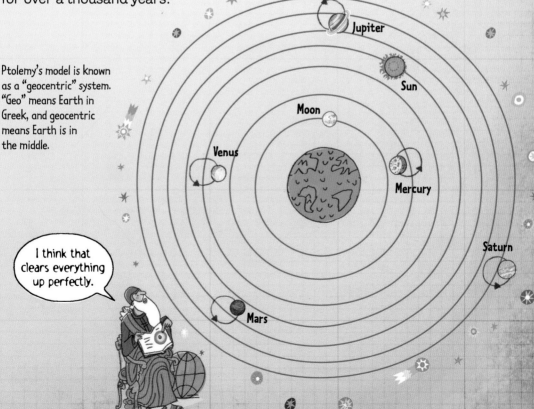

I think that clears everything up perfectly.

Jupiter

Sun

Moon

Venus

Mercury

Saturn

Mars

Middle Eastern astronomy

Ancient Greek astronomy had a big influence on the astronomers who lived in the area now known as the Middle East. During the 8th and 9th centuries, scholars there translated all kinds of Greek ideas.

It was a time when mathematics and astronomy flourished and astronomical instruments such as quadrants (used for measuring the positions of stars) became more sophisticated.

Early science fiction

Stories about journeys to other worlds became popular centuries before space travel was possible.

In the 2nd century, around the time of Ptolemy, a writer from ancient Turkey named Lucian wrote stories about aliens and space travel.

The tales starred bizarre characters, such as soldiers who flew on giant insects, Moon-dwellers with tails made of cabbage, and dog-faced men from the star known as Sirius.

This is a painting of Middle Eastern astronomers using various tools to help them measure the height of stars and do calculations based on their observations of the skies.

The Muslim rulers of the area – the Caliphs – built observatories, usually on hills, to make stargazing easier. These were stocked with instruments and books, and often used for teaching young astronomers.

Stargazers in cities such as Baghdad could predict movements of the Sun, Moon and planets more accurately than Ptolemy had done. This was very useful for Muslims, whose prayer times are based on the Sun's movements.

A revolution in the sky

Greek and Middle Eastern ideas were passed on to Europe in the 13th and 14th centuries.

In the 16th century, a Polish clergyman known as Copernicus started to pick holes in Ptolemy's theories. Ptolemy had been forced to come up with fiendishly complicated rules to make the movements of the planets fit his geocentric system.

Copernicus wondered if there was a simpler explanation. What if the Sun was in the middle? This might explain why the planets seemed to change direction. As Earth whizzed past a slower planet, that planet would seem to go back on itself.

This is an astrolabe – a type of astronomical instrument invented by the Greeks and improved upon by Middle Eastern astronomers.

Astrolabes had rotating plates that acted as moving maps of the stars. They had lots of different uses, including telling the time.

This diagram shows what Copernicus thought the Universe looked like. Later, astronomers calculated that the planets moved in ovals, not circles.

A not-so-perfect world

Ptolemy also believed that the sky was perfect and its movements never changed. But in 1572, the Danish astronomer, Tycho Brahe, spotted what he thought was a new star. Actually, it was a supernova, and it disappeared a few months later. If stars could appear and then vanish, how could the sky be unchanging? Ptolemy's system was looking less and less convincing.

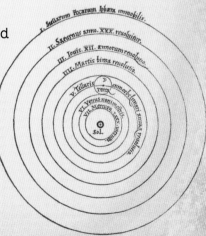

Made by kids?

Some stories say that the idea for the first telescope came to its inventor, Hans Lippershey, after watching his children fiddling around with glass spectacle lenses.

When they held up two lenses at once and looked through them, they noticed that they could see a weather vane on a nearby church steeple much more clearly.

The invention of the telescope

In the 17th century, a new invention came along that changed astronomy forever: the telescope. For the first time, astronomers had a tool that could make the stars look clearer and closer.

It's not certain who made the first one, but the person who usually gets the credit – Hans Lippershey – was a spectacle-maker, not an astronomer. In 1608, he discovered that lining up two glass lenses at each end of a tube made objects seem closer.

At first, people thought the device would be used in battles, to spy on enemy soldiers from a distance. But it wasn't long before an astronomer realized how handy it could be for stargazing.

Galileo gets a closer look

The first astronomer to use a telescope to scan the skies was an Italian named Galileo Galilei. He was a skilled craftsman and, as soon as he heard about the new invention, he set about making his own – and making it better. He eventually created a gadget that could magnify objects about twenty times.

He got a lot of praise for his achievement. The name telescope was actually thought up by someone at a party being held for Galileo.

This diagram shows you how light passed through Galileo's telescope. The lenses focus the light.

Eyepiece lens

Eye

Light from the sky

Objective lens

Object being looked at, such as a star

Copernicus was right

When Galileo peered through his telescope, he was amazed by what he saw. There were moons orbiting Jupiter, and mountains and valleys on the surface of the Moon. But, most importantly, he saw that Venus had phases, like the Moon. That doesn't sound dramatic, but it showed that Venus must be orbiting the Sun, not Earth.

So, Earth couldn't be at the middle of everything after all. Before looking through the telescope, Galileo had thought that Copernicus was probably right. But now he had the evidence of his own eyes.

What keeps the Universe together?

Another thing still puzzled astronomers – why didn't the planets float away? What kept them in orbit?

A man named Isaac Newton solved this mystery in the 1660s, with his theory that all objects attract each other with a pulling force. He named this force gravity, from the Latin for weight.

Newton also built telescopes. He improved on Galileo's designs by using mirrors, not lenses, giving clearer, brighter images.

Galileo's design sometimes gave objects a violet halo. Newton's mirror-based telescope helped to solve this problem.

Astronomy on trial

Galileo got in trouble with the Catholic Church when he published a book saying that the Earth went round the Sun.

The Church believed that Earth was in the middle of a perfect Universe. Going against that was a crime against God.

In 1633, Galileo was put on trial and made to take back what he said. He did, but he still knew he was right.

Newton's inspiration

Some stories say that Newton came up with his theory of gravity when an apple fell on his head.

It didn't happen quite like that – it took him a long time to piece together his ideas. But he certainly wrote about wondering why apples fell off the trees in his garden.

Eyepiece lens

Eye

Secondary mirror

Primary mirror

Stop my sailors from getting lost, will you?

Bigger and better telescopes

After Newton, astronomers built telescopes that gave even clearer views of space. William Herschel even managed to spot a new planet using a telescope he had built, although at first he thought it was a comet.

Royal astronomy

In 1675, King Charles II hired an Astronomer Royal, whose job was to make star maps to help sailors navigate.

Getting lost meant losing battles for the navy, so it was vital work.

Britain still has an Astronomer Royal today.

In the 1700s, James Short became one of the first professional telescope makers.

William Herschel used a telescope like this one to discover Uranus in 1781.

Some monstrously huge telescopes were built. These gave greater magnification, but they weren't always practical because they couldn't be moved.

In 1845, a wealthy mathematician named William Parsons (also known as Lord Rosse) created a gigantic telescope which many astronomers used to map the Moon's craters and to view never-before-seen stars.

More than man-sized

When the Rosse telescope was officially opened, a man walked through its tube wearing a top hat and carrying an umbrella above his head, to give a sense of just how immense the instrument was.

On the right is the enormous Rosse telescope. To use it you had to stand on a platform high above the ground.

The Universe gets bigger too

In 1923, an American astronomer named Edwin Hubble used an enormous telescope to identify other galaxies, millions of light years away. Before that, astronomers had thought our Milky Way *was* the Universe. Imagine thinking your country is the only one, then discovering millions of others. Hubble also calculated that other galaxies were moving away from us faster and faster. The Universe was expanding.

A new theory of gravity

About this time, a scientist named Albert Einstein realized that Newton's theory of gravity didn't always explain how objects behaved in space. He published his own theory in 1916, which explained that huge objects, such as planets, make space curve, so other objects fall in their direction.

But soon, scientists weren't just coming up with theories about space. They actually had the technology to send people out there to explore.

How far are the stars?

In 1838, a German named Friedrich Bessel was the first person to measure the distance to one of the stars – 61 Cygni.

He used a method called parallax – measuring how a star's position seems to shift over a year, compared to the other stars. Bessel estimated, fairly accurately, that Cygni was 100 trillion km (62 trillion miles) away.

This is the Hooker telescope at Mount Wilson Observatory in California. Hubble used it to reveal the true nature of other galaxies.

Time travel?

Einstein said that time could change speed depending on how fast you went compared to someone else.

Imagine a woman zooming through space in a spaceship at almost the speed of light, while her twin stays behind.

When she returns, her twin will be older than her. This is because time moves slower on Earth than it does for someone going much faster.

Don't worry if you're baffled. Even scientists find my ideas tricky.

Chapter 5

A race into space

Since ancient times, people have dreamed of visiting other worlds, but it wasn't until the 1950s that those dreams started to become a reality. Getting into space became an obsession for two powerful nations – the United States and the Soviet Union (the former name for Russia and many of the smaller countries surrounding it).

Both spent vast sums of money on spaceships. First, they launched robot craft, then living creatures, and then, finally, humans. And humans didn't just fly into space. They went all the way to the Moon.

This photo shows an astronaut named Edward "Buzz" Aldrin on the Moon in 1969. You can see another astronaut, Neil Armstrong, reflected in his visor.

An old Chinese story dating back to the 1500s tells of a man named Wan Hu who tried to launch himself into space using rockets powered by gunpowder.

Wan Hu, the story goes, attached firework-like rockets to a chair and sat down in it. As the rockets were lit, there was a bang. When the smoke cleared, Wan Hu was nowhere to be seen...

from bombs to spaceships

To get to outer space, you have to zoom up at thousands of miles an hour to make up for the fact that gravity is slowing you down.

People have known for centuries that you have to go really fast to get into space. But gravity-cheating speeds only became possible when rocket technology was developed in the 20th century.

Rockets work by forcing hot gas out through thrusters at the bottom, pushing the rocket up. During the Second World War, scientists built rockets with bombs in, but they also used rockets (minus the exploding part) to try to get into space. In 1942, a German *V-2* rocket reached the edge of Earth's atmosphere. Outer space was finally within reach.

A lap around Earth

In 1957, the Russians successfully launched a rocket into outer space. Mounted on this rocket was a tiny craft called *Sputnik 1* – a hollow metal ball, about the size of a beach ball, with a radio transmitter and other gadgets inside.

When it got far enough into space, the rocket fell away, and *Sputnik* orbited Earth alone. Russian scientists down on Earth were overjoyed to hear the "beep, beep, beep," of *Sputnik*'s transmitter over their radios.

This is a replica of *Sputnik 1*. The real thing was destroyed when it hit the Earth's atmosphere.

The Space Race begins

Sputnik 1 was the first man-made "satellite" – that is, an object that orbits another in space. But it wasn't just a first for humankind. It was a victory for the Russians over their rivals, the Americans.

Both the Soviet Union and the USA believed that conquering space would prove how powerful they were. This scramble into the sky became known as the Space Race. By launching *Sputnik*, the Russians had won the first lap.

Laika the spacedog

Later that year, a second *Sputnik* craft was launched with a passenger – a dog named Laika, which means "barker" in Russian. Laika endured months of harsh tests in machines that imitated conditions in space.

Laika stayed calm all through her training sessions and, when *Sputnik 2* launched, she made a successful orbit of Earth. But her journey only lasted a few hours. Sadly, Laika died when her cabin got too hot.

A mini metal moon

Our Moon is a natural satellite – an object that orbits another object in space.

As Earth's first man-made satellite, *Sputnik 1* joined the Moon in orbit, although its orbit was much smaller.

The little ship made about 1,400 orbits and was sometimes visible through binoculars or telescopes or even the naked eye. Some eager astronomers tracked its path through the sky.

Animals in space

In 1970, two frogs were sent into space to study the effects of motion sickness in spaceships. Frogs were used because their ears are quite like ours, and it's the parts inside our ears that give us a sense of balance.

All kinds of creatures have gone into space, including cats, tortoises, rats and flies.

Astropups

In 1960, the Russians sent two dogs, Strelka and Belka, into orbit and brought them home safe and sound.

The Russian leader at the time, a man named Nikita Khrushchev, gave a present of one of Strelka's puppies to the daughter of the US President, John F. Kennedy.

Ham the Chimp-o-naut

The next question was, could a living creature carry out tasks in space? In 1961, the Americans trained a chimp named Ham to pull levers, using bananas as rewards and electric shocks as punishments. Ham repeated his tasks in space and returned safely, too.

This is Ham with one of his keepers.

Space dummy

In 1961, Russians sent up a lifeless dummy in a spacesuit to test that the suit – and other equipment that a human astronaut was going to use – worked OK.

The dummy was named Ivan Ivanovich and was made to look very lifelike. It had eyes, eyebrows, eyelashes and a mouth.

In case anyone found Ivan when he landed and thought he was a dead body or an alien, they wrote "MAKET" – Russian for "dummy" – on his face.

Training for the Space Race

It was time to put a human into space. Both nations put their best military pilots through endless fitness tests, as well as written exams and special training to deal with the strange conditions in space.

For example, American would-be astronauts trained in a plane that flew up and down very fast, so they felt as if they were floating. It was nicknamed the "vomit comet" – you can probably guess why.

The first spaceman

The first person to fly into orbit was a Russian named Yuri Gagarin. It was a dangerous trip, as no one knew what the effects of space flight would be on a human.

I'm not dead, I'm a dummy.

We have lift-off!

On April 12, 1961, Yuri was strapped into the cabin of a spacecraft named *Vostok 1*. The cabin was just large enough to hold Yuri, plus the equipment he'd need.

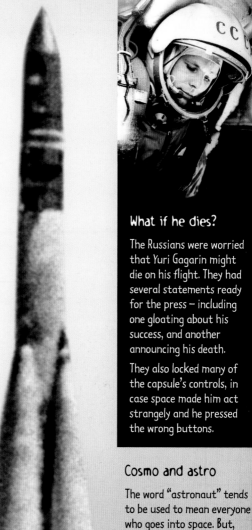

Antennae to transmit radio signals

Oxygen tanks and instruments went here.

Yuri sat inside a small capsule, on an ejector seat.

That morning, *Vostok 1* blasted off, attached to a launch rocket. Yuri cried out over his radio, "We're off!" He made it safely into space, circling Earth at a speed of 27,400 km/h (16,777 mph) on a flight that lasted 108 minutes.

    Peering below him as he orbited the planet, he said, "I see Earth. It's so beautiful!"

    After he zoomed back down into the atmosphere, Yuri activated his ejector seat and parachuted safely to Earth.

What if he dies?

The Russians were worried that Yuri Gagarin might die on his flight. They had several statements ready for the press — including one gloating about his success, and another announcing his death.

They also locked many of the capsule's controls, in case space made him act strangely and he pressed the wrong buttons.

Cosmo and astro

The word "astronaut" tends to be used to mean everyone who goes into space. But, technically speaking, people who go into space aren't *all* astronauts.

    American space voyagers, or people who go into space on American craft, are known as astronauts. But Russian space voyagers, or people who've gone to space on Russian craft, are known as cosmonauts.

2nd place goes to...

The second person in space was an American named Alan Shepard.

On May 5, 1961, he flew up about 200km (115 miles) in the *Freedom 7* spacecraft. He didn't orbit Earth or go as far as Yuri Gagarin, but he became the first person to return to Earth inside his spaceship, splashing down into the sea.

The President's promise

The Americans were stunned at being beaten into space by the Russians, but it made them even more determined to get to the Moon first.

That same year, 1961, the American President, John F. Kennedy, made a speech promising to put a man on the Moon before the end of the decade. His promise was fulfilled with months to spare.

On July 16th 1969, a huge rocket blasted off into space, carrying a craft with three Americans on board – Michael Collins, Neil Armstrong and Edwin "Buzz" Aldrin. Their mission's name was *Apollo 11*, and the world waited eagerly to see if it would succeed.

Four days later, the *Apollo 11* team reached the Moon's orbit. Michael stayed on the command module, while Neil and Buzz flew down to the surface in a landing craft known as the *Eagle*.

This is Buzz Aldrin taking a walk on the surface of the Moon, near the *Eagle*.

Walking on another world

As Neil climbed slowly down the *Eagle*'s ladder to the surface of the Moon, he announced, "That's one small step for man, one giant leap for mankind."

Back on Earth, over 600 million people were glued to their television screens as Neil took the first, bouncing steps on the the Moon, protected from the cold and airless world by his spacesuit. Although his suit was heavy, the gravity on the Moon is weak, so he almost seemed to fly through the air.

The Americans had won a great victory and the *Apollo* astronauts went home as heroes.

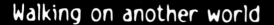

Planting the flag

Neil Armstrong and Buzz Aldrin spent about two hours outside on the surface of the Moon.

During this time, they planted an American flag, collected soil samples and took photos. These were printed in newspapers all over the world.

Friends at last

The Americans and the Russians were enemies for many years, but eventually they patched things up enough to work together in space.

In 1975, an American and a Russian spacecraft linked up. By the 1990s, cosmonauts and astronauts were living and working together in space.

This astronaut is strapped to a robot arm that's part of the International Space Station.

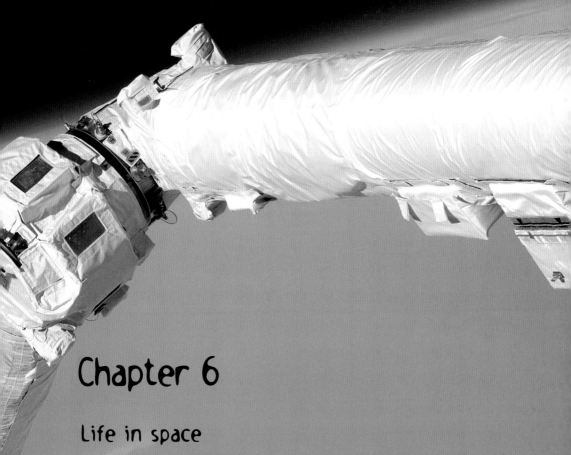

Chapter 6

Life in space

Today, astronauts from all over the world blast off into space. Some even stay out there for months. Many modern astronauts are trained scientists who spend time in space doing experiments on space stations in constant orbit around the Earth.

What's it like to spend your working days floating around or slipping into a sealed suit and taking a walk in the airless void of space? How do you get to be an astronaut? And how do people eat, sleep and use the toilet in space?

Who goes to space now?

Astronauts from all over the
globe now fly into space on
Russian and American crafts as
passengers. China has its own
crafts, too.

American NASA Space
Shuttle on a rocket

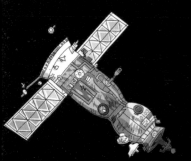

Russian Soyuz
craft

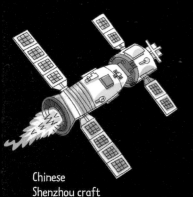

Chinese
Shenzhou craft

What's space travel like today?

When Yuri Gagarin first blasted into space, he said
it felt as if a heavy weight was pressing on him, like
the feeling you get when a car speeds up, only much,
much stronger. Technology has moved on, but the
two minutes after launch are still a noisy, shaky ride.

A few minutes after a spaceship blasts into space,
its rockets drop off and the ride gets smoother.

Once in orbit, astronauts experience something
known as zero gravity or microgravity. This makes
them feel as if they're floating, but they're actually
falling. A ship in orbit is always falling in the direction
of Earth, tugged by the planet's gravity. Its speed
makes up for this tug, so it stays in orbit.

Some astronauts stay in space for months, on
ships called space stations. There have been a few of
these but the one up there now is the International
Space Station (ISS). It orbits us about 16 times a day,
400 km (250 miles) up.

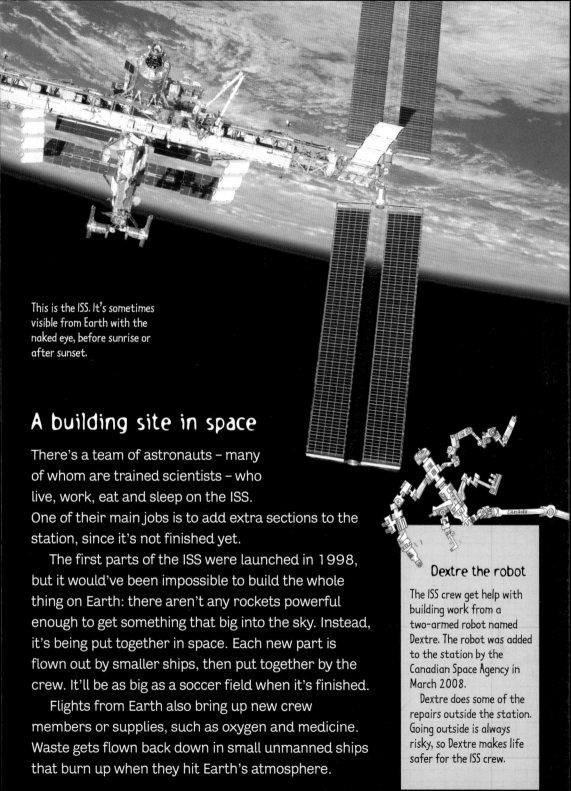

This is the ISS. It's sometimes visible from Earth with the naked eye, before sunrise or after sunset.

A building site in space

There's a team of astronauts – many of whom are trained scientists – who live, work, eat and sleep on the ISS. One of their main jobs is to add extra sections to the station, since it's not finished yet.

The first parts of the ISS were launched in 1998, but it would've been impossible to build the whole thing on Earth: there aren't any rockets powerful enough to get something that big into the sky. Instead, it's being put together in space. Each new part is flown out by smaller ships, then put together by the crew. It'll be as big as a soccer field when it's finished.

Flights from Earth also bring up new crew members or supplies, such as oxygen and medicine. Waste gets flown back down in small unmanned ships that burn up when they hit Earth's atmosphere.

Dextre the robot

The ISS crew get help with building work from a two-armed robot named Dextre. The robot was added to the station by the Canadian Space Agency in March 2008.

Dextre does some of the repairs outside the station. Going outside is always risky, so Dextre makes life safer for the ISS crew.

Training to be an astronaut

Astronauts usually train for years before they go into space.

Many study science, mathematics or engineering, as well as taking special astronaut exams.

You have to be tough to live in the strange conditions of space. So astronauts have to pass lots of physical tests to prove they're up to it.

They also train in space-like conditions – for example, they use machines that make it feel as if they're in zero gravity.

How much does space travel cost?

Putting astronauts in space and keeping them there costs billions of dollars.

Just sending up the NASA Space Shuttle costs around $450 million each time. It even costs $5,000 to ship a kilogram of water to the ISS.

Still, governments spend a lot more on other things. The US government, for example, spends less than 1% of its money on NASA projects.

Daily (and nightly) life on board

Day and night don't mean much on board the ISS. The station circles Earth every 90 minutes, so the crew members experience 15 dawns every 24 hours.

They do try to keep to normal sleep patterns, but they don't sleep in beds. There are a few little cabins, but the astronauts can sleep almost anywhere as long as they attach their sleeping bag so they don't float around, bumping into things.

You can breathe normally on the ISS, as the station has its own air supply. But in space your body doesn't behave as it does in normal gravity. For example, when you're getting dressed, you might find that your arm is floating above your head instead of going into your sleeve.

Meals are tricky, too. Drinks and soups have to be sucked from plastic bags, through straws. The sauce on solid food has to be very sticky so it doesn't escape and the food itself can't be too crumbly. If crumbs floated away, it would be impossible to clean them up.

Working on the ISS

Much of the day is spent doing scientific experiments. The crew does tests to see how being in space affects objects, plants and people. Because they're working in zero gravity, they have to use restraints to stop themselves or their equipment from floating away.

Their experiments teach scientists more about how the human body works in space, and might help humans make longer space voyages in the future.

A drafty toilet

On Earth, toilets rely on gravity to flush. If you used a normal toilet in space, the water – and everything else – would float around in the air. To avoid this yucky experience, toilets in space use a vacuum cleaner-like machine to suck everything up instead.

The urine is then recycled into drinking water. That may sound disgusting, but once purified, it's actually very clean.

Breathing on the ISS

The ISS – and other manned spaceships – have a mechanical life support system that provides the crew with air.

This also keeps the temperature steady and does other tasks that keep the crew alive and comfy, such as providing clean water.

Some of the air comes from tanks of oxygen, but some is made on board using water, since water contains oxygen.

This astronaut is using an exercise machine on the ISS.

Bodies in space

Strange things happen to your body when you spend a while in space. On Earth, gravity is always pushing down on your spine, but the lack of gravity in space means your bones get weaker, and you get taller, too.

On Earth, you use your muscles just to stay standing or sitting. But in space, astronauts need to work out on exercise machines for at least 2½ hours a day just to keep their muscles from wasting away.

A space vacation

You don't have to be an astronaut to go into space. You just have to have enough money.

A tour company will soon be taking people on day trips into space. A two-hour flight will cost around $200,000 and take passengers 100 km (62 miles) above Earth.

Passengers will experience weightlessness and take in amazing views of Earth and space.

How spacesuits work

Spacesuits have lots of layers to protect astronauts from heat, cold, and the Sun's radiation. The atmosphere shields us from this on Earth.

Each spacesuit has an air supply, plus microphones and earphones for communicating with the main spacecraft.

Space walks can last hours, so astronauts have to wear special underpants to collect their urine.

Oxygen to breathe

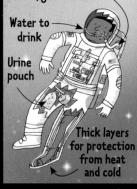

Water to drink

Urine pouch

Thick layers for protection from heat and cold

When astronauts go on EVA, they are usually tied to their craft by a cable to keep them from floating away.

Going on a space walk

Going for a walk outside a spaceship is known as Extra Vehicular Activity, or EVA. It's a tricky task, because space is a very hostile place.

To go on an EVA, you need a spacesuit to provide you with air to breathe and protect you from the cold – or extreme heat, if the Sun's shining on you. It can go down to about -160 °C (-258 °F) in the shadows and up to about +120 °C (+248 °F) in the light. A spacesuit also needs to protect against the Sun's deadly radiation and dazzling glare. So spacesuits are designed to block radiation, with visors to protect the wearer's eyes.

Even opening the door is complicated. Space stations have "airlocks" – doors that stop air from escaping into space.

A dangerous vacuum

Space is a vacuum – a place where there's no air. This is dangerous, and not just because you can't breathe there. On Earth, or in a spacecraft, the air presses on you. This is known as air pressure. But there isn't any in space. Even in a spacesuit, the pressure's quite low.

If you move too quickly between different pressures you can get a painful illness called "the bends" – deep sea divers get it when they come up too quickly. To avoid this, astronauts spend hours in the airlock before an EVA, where the pressure is lowered slowly, so their bodies can adjust.

Spaceships of the future

In about 2015, the NASA Space Shuttles will be replaced by a new kind of vehicle known as *Orion*. These craft will look like older designs, such as the *Apollo 11* ships, but they'll be roomier and far more hi-tech. The Shuttles are going to stop running before the *Orion* ships are ready, so NASA astronauts will have to find another way to reach the ISS in the meantime – perhaps hitch a lift on a Russian craft?

Travel to other planets isn't possible yet. Any ship going farther than the Moon would have to be so big – to fit in enough supplies – that it'd be too heavy to launch. It'd have to be built in space or on the Moon.

But the main problem is the length of the trip. People who stay in space for over 100 days come back in a terrible state, with weak bones and muscles. The trip to, say, Mars would take over 250 days. Still, the research being done on the ISS may help find a solution to this problem.

Burning up

Coming back into Earth's atmosphere is known as re-entry. During this, the air around a spaceship gets very hot. Any ship that's not heat-resistant enough could burn up.

In 2003, a Space Shuttle named *Columbia* broke apart after the heat-resistant tiles on the outside were damaged. The seven people on board were killed.

Bases on the Moon

No one has built a base on the Moon (or an alien planet) yet. But NASA plans to start building a base on the Moon where scientists could live and work by about 2020.

Ships could stop off there on their way to other planets, too.

These dishes — at the New Mexico site of the National Radio Astronomy Observatory — are known as the Very Large Array. They're used to pick up invisible light that some stars give off.

Chapter 7

Telescopes and other technology

Modern space technology can do some amazing things. There's a flying telescope in orbit around the planet right now, which sends back photos of distant corners of the Universe. Farther away, robots are flying to other planets to do experiments that will teach us more about alien worlds. Meanwhile, on Earth, astronomers are using powerful telescopes to learn more and more about the Universe.

Powering a telescope in space

The Hubble Space telescope is powered by energy from the Sun. When sunlight hits its shiny solar panels, the heat and light are turned into electricity.

When Hubble is in Earth's shadow, the telescope runs on batteries. These are recharged when Hubble's in sunlight.

Does Hubble ever point at Earth?

In theory, the Hubble Space Telescope could be turned to look at Earth, but it's unlikely that it will be.

For a start, astronomers are obviously more interested in the stars.

But even if they wanted to point Hubble at Earth, it's too risky. Hubble's instruments are very sensitive. Earth reflects a lot of light from the Sun, so Hubble might be damaged by its glare.

A flying telescope

There's a telescope the size of a school bus flying in orbit beyond the ISS. It's called the Hubble Space Telescope. There are actually a few telescopes out in space, but Hubble is the most famous, thanks to the spectacular pictures that it takes.

Scientists control it from Earth, sending messages to its on-board computer, telling it where to point. Hubble's cameras send back images as information, which scientists then turn into pictures.

How does Hubble work?

Like many telescopes on Earth, Hubble uses mirrors to gather light. Usually, the larger the mirror, the clearer your view of space. But Hubble's mirror, which is about 2.4m (8ft) across, isn't as large as the ones in some Earth telescopes: it doesn't need to be.

Earth telescopes have to peer through the atmosphere to look into space. As the light from stars moves through the air, it jiggles around, which is why stars twinkle. This twinkling blurs the images seen through Earth telescopes. But, in space, there's no atmosphere, so Hubble gets an unspoiled view.

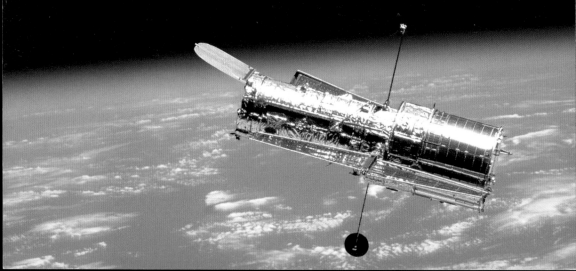

What can Hubble do?

Hubble shows us views of the Universe that were never possible before – from images of stars surrounded by dust that might someday turn into another solar system, to pictures of galaxies colliding. It can take photographs of objects that are 50 times fainter than anything visible from Earth.

In fact, Hubble can see some of the most distant known objects in the Universe, about 13 billion light years away. That means some of the light that Hubble picks up is almost as old as the Universe itself.

New discoveries

In 2006, Hubble discovered 16 new planets orbiting distant stars in our Galaxy. It did this by peering at 180,000 stars in a crowded part of the Galaxy, using its "Advanced Camera for Surveys" – ACS for short.

The planets were too far away to view directly, so astronomers used the ACS to measure the slight dimming that happens to a star when a planet passes in front of it.

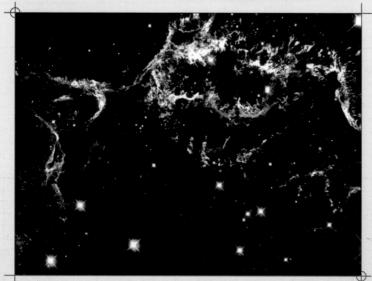

This image, captured by one of Hubble's cameras, shows the remains of a dead star, 10,000 light years from Earth.

What's a black hole?

A black hole is a space object that has a lot of matter in an incredibly small space. Its powerful gravity sucks in everything nearby, even light.

Seeing invisible things

Hubble has a "spectrograph" on board – a gadget used to study light. This has given astronomers vital clues about some of the Universe's strangest objects – from things called black holes, to invisible "dark" energy and matter. These things can't be seen, but Hubble has helped scientists study how they affect nearby objects.

You can't see black holes themselves. But scientists can locate them by the way their gravity pulls on nearby space dust and stars.

Robot explorers

It's too dangerous and expensive to send humans to other planets just yet. In the meantime, remote-controlled machines fly to other planets and moons to beam back photos and other information.

Some of these orbit or fly past planets as far away as Neptune. Others have actually landed on other worlds – on Venus, Titan (one of Saturn's moons) and Mars. Mars is the most-visited planet in the Solar System, with six ships making successful landings.

In 2004, two identical robots, named *Spirit* and *Opportunity*, arrived on Mars. These little wheeled "rover" robots left their landing craft and trundled onto the planet's surface. Using photos taken by the rovers to guide them, scientists back on Earth steered the robots around slowly and safely, investigating rocks and sifting through soil.

The rovers have sent back stunning images of Martian sunsets, whirling dust storms and clouds drifting through the planet's sky.

Robonaut

NASA has built a robot astronaut that can use screwdrivers and do many of the tasks that human astronauts normally do.

It's still being tested so it hasn't been to space just yet.

This is an artist's impression of the *Spirit* rover on Mars. Scientists hoped the rovers would last three months after landing. But the tough little robots were still driving around four years later.

The great alien hunt

No human has ever set foot on an alien planet. But have aliens visited ours? Most scientists think not, although intelligent life might exist on distant planets. Maybe they're wondering if we exist too?

In the 1960s, scientists started sending out signals into space – from pieces of music to mathematical equations – hoping that aliens would pick them up and get in touch.

Probes have also been sent out carrying information, such as pictures of humans and star charts showing how to get to our planet.

There's an organization that hunts for alien life called the Search for Extra-Terrestrial Intelligence (SETI). It studies information from telescopes and other space-scanning devices that might be able to pick up messages from aliens.

Alien abductions?

Many people believe they've seen aliens, or even been abducted by them.

Some say they've been taken to laboratories where the aliens experimented on them. But it's possible that these were hallucinations – the human mind can play powerful tricks sometimes.

Spying from space

Even if there aren't any aliens, space is still very busy. There are thousands of man-made, computer-controlled satellites circling the planet.

Every day, signals are beamed from Earth and bounced off communications and broadcast satellites, back down to another part of the planet. This transmits television signals and other information, such as telephone calls, all over the world.

Weather satellites and other scientific satellites study our planet and space. Mysterious spy satellites orbit the planet to observe enemy movements, photograph military bases and give early warnings of missile launches, among other top secret tasks.

Junk in orbit

Not all man-made satellites do useful jobs. Lots of floating pieces of space junk have also been pulled into orbit.

These include nuts and bolts that astronauts have dropped while repairing space ships, old batteries and parts of rockets that were used to launch crafts into orbit.

This junk could be a danger to spaceships, as it whizzes through space.

Space spin-offs

All these inventions are based on technology that was first developed for space travel:

- Pens that write upside-down
- Satellite navigation for cars
- Flat screen televisions
- Voice-activated wheelchairs
- Shock absorbing running shoes
- Invisible teeth braces
- Sleep suits for babies that warn their parents if they stop breathing
- Non-stick frying pans

Astronomy on Earth

Many of the telescopes that professional astronomers use are basically huge cameras, and the pictures they take are viewed on computer screens. Other telescopes gather information which is then displayed as a chart or a graph. So, many professional astronomers spend a lot of time studying wiggly lines on monitors rather than observing the skies directly.

Amateurs tend to stargaze the traditional way, peering up through telescopes, although some do hook their telescopes up to cameras or computers.

High up telescopes

The largest telescopes on Earth can cost millions and millions and can see billions of light years into space. They're usually housed in observatories, high up on mountains and away from the glare of city lights. Observatories are stocked with computers and other instruments as well as huge telescopes.

The Keck Observatory is 4km (2.5 miles) up a mountain in Hawaii. It houses the world's largest reflector telescopes.

Making pictures with light

The reason we can see stars in the sky is because they give off light. The telescopes that gather this light are known as optical telescopes, and there are three main types: refractors, reflectors and compound telescopes.

Refractors use lenses to gather and focus light, while reflectors use mirrors instead. Compound telescopes use a combination of mirrors and lenses.

Each type of telescope has its own advantages. For example, if you compare a refractor and a reflector of the same size, the refractor would usually be better for giving a clear image of bright objects such as planets. The reflector would (usually) be better for viewing fainter things such as nebulae.

A refractor telescope

Telescope tip

If you want to buy your own telescope, you can find out more about the different kinds on the Usborne Quicklinks Website – see the start of the book for more details.

One important thing to bear in mind is that the usefulness of a telescope depends on the size of its mirror or lens. Larger ones gather more light, so you can see the stars more clearly.

Signals from the stars

Some professional astronomers use huge, dish-shaped "radio" telescopes, which pick up an invisible kind of light known as radio waves. As the name suggests, radio waves are what make radios work, but they also occur naturally.

Many objects in space, such as stars and galaxies, give off radio waves and other invisible types of light. By studying these, astronomers can learn more about the objects that give them off. Astronomers also turn radio waves into images using computers, so we can see parts of space that would be otherwise invisible.

This is what the Sun and the Earth will probably look like in about five billion years' time. The Earth will be dry and dead and the Sun will be huge.

Chapter 8

The story of the Universe

Billions of years ago, at the beginning of the
Universe, there was nothing. Not the everyday
kind of nothing that you'd find in an empty box,
because an empty box still takes up space. At the
start of everything, there wasn't even any space.

How did we get from nothingness to a Universe
full of shining stars and spinning planets? And
what will happen to our Universe as it gets older?

Science fiction movies are full of scary ways
for the world to end, from alien invasions to
disgusting plagues, but what will really happen?
Will we be bashed out of the sky by an asteroid?
Will the whole Universe be destroyed one day?
One thing is almost certain – our precious, wet
little planet will some day come to an end.

Space timeline

This is (roughly) how the Universe's life story has gone so far.

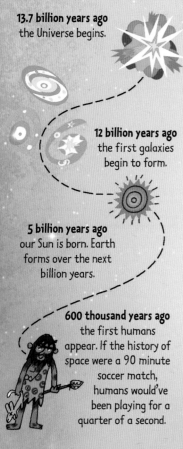

13.7 billion years ago the Universe begins.

12 billion years ago the first galaxies begin to form.

5 billion years ago our Sun is born. Earth forms over the next billion years.

600 thousand years ago the first humans appear. If the history of space were a 90 minute soccer match, humans would've been playing for a quarter of a second.

A ridiculous idea

An astronomer named Fred Hoyle gave the Big Bang theory its name.

He actually thought it was a load of nonsense but when he called it a "Big Bang" in a radio interview, the name stuck.

Once upon a time...

...there was nothing at all. No Earth, no Sun, no light or dark. Nothing whatsoever – a hard thing to imagine, when you're used to today's busy, jam-packed Universe.

But one day, about 13.7 billion years ago, a tiny speck popped into existence. It was thousands of times smaller than the head of a pin, and hotter and denser than anything that has ever been since.

This speck contained all the stuff that has ever existed in the Universe. It exploded out in all directions so quickly that, within a second, it was already bigger than a galaxy.

The Universe explodes

Scientists call this strange, sudden beginning the Big Bang. The name makes it sound noisy, but actually it would have been silent. Things were expanding so quickly that sound simply couldn't have kept up – even if there had been any air to carry the sound.

In its first moments, the Universe became a blisteringly hot fireball. As this ball spread out, it cooled down and separated out into lumps of matter.

After this speedy start, it took another billion years or so before these lumps joined together to make the first stars. Our own Sun started to form about 5 billion years ago.

It's thought that the Sun and our entire Solar System is made up of dust and gas that came from an exploding supernova star. So the Sun, Earth, and everything on it is made of stardust – even you.

How do we know what happened?

The simple answer is we don't. Most scientists now agree that the Big Bang *did* happen, but there's still a lot we don't know about how the Universe began.

The Big Bang idea developed in the 1940s, after Hubble realized that the Universe was expanding. If it's getting bigger, scientists reasoned, it must've been smaller before. So perhaps it once wasn't there at all?

To learn more about the Big Bang, scientists at one of the world's largest laboratories have built a massive machine called the Large Hadron Collider or LHC. This is designed to recreate the conditions that would have existed just after the Big Bang.

Before this machine was turned on in August 2008, lots of newspaper headlines claimed that it might create a black hole and end the world. (It didn't.)

What shape is the Universe?

The Universe's shape remains a mystery. Some scientists believe it's round like a ball.

Others say it's more like a ring or a tube. Some scientists claim there is a "multiverse", made up of many universes – each one slightly different.

This machine is called the Large Hadron Collider or LHC, is at the CERN laboratory on the border of France and Switzerland..

The end isn't very nigh

One day, all this will be gone: the book in your hands, the planet under your feet, not to mention your feet themselves. One day, the Sun will die and all life on Earth will be wiped out. Worried?

You shouldn't be, because Earth will be sticking around for a long while yet. By the time the Sun dies, your great, great, great, great, great, great (and many greats after that) grandchildren will be dead.

A scary old giant

Scientists think the Sun will die in about five billion years. But, before it reaches the end of its life, the Sun will start to get bigger and turn into a red giant. It may become 200 times bigger than it is now.

As it swells to a monstrous size, Mercury and Venus will be swallowed up. On our planet, the temperature will shoot up and all the water in the oceans will sizzle away – which will mean bye bye life on Earth.

Scientists aren't sure whether Earth will be swallowed too. If its orbit gets bigger, it might not, and it's the Sun that might help it make its escape.

As the Sun swells, it will lose some of its mass. This may sound odd. Why would its mass get smaller if it's getting bigger?

It's because the Sun will throw its outer layers of gas into space as it gets cooler. So, although the Sun will take up more room, there will be less matter in it. As its mass gets smaller, the tug of its gravity will get weaker, too. Then, Earth might be able to escape into a larger orbit and avoid becoming a snack for a hungry red giant.

Ways that we could be wiped out before the Sun kills us

- A massive comet or asteroid could crash into us.
- The Moon could be struck by a comet or asteroid, raining debris on our planet.
- Humans might kill themselves by polluting Earth, creating a killer virus, or starting a nuclear war.
- A flash of radiation far away in space, known as a gamma ray burst, could destroy the atmosphere and kill anything that lives on land.

Shh, don't mention the end of the world

It's not going to happen for millions of years but people can still be touchy about it.

Once, when famous scientist Stephen Hawking was giving a lecture, he was asked not to mention the end of the world in case it made people panic.

Living on other worlds

If humans survive long enough, we'll need to find a new home before Earth is barbecued. We could build vast space stations, big enough to grow crops, or move to a planet that's farther from the Sun. Or we could find a planet in orbit around another star.

It's unlikely that we'll find a world with *exactly* the same conditions as Earth. But we could artificially alter its atmosphere and climate (known as "terraforming") or build sealed cities, where air could be made using gases in the planet's atmosphere.

Pricey planets

We don't have the technology yet to live on other planets or to build space stations that would support life forever.

This is partly because it's too expensive. But if Earth was ever threatened by disaster, governments would be sure to spend whatever it took to make a home in space for at least some of the human race.

In the future, we could build domed cities like this one on other planets or moons.

Will the Universe ever end?

No one can be sure what'll happen when the Universe gets very old. Some scientists think it might collapse, getting smaller until it's squished out of existence in a "Big Crunch" – the opposite of the Big Bang.

But it's most likely that the galaxies will keep on rushing apart until you can't see one galaxy from another. Our Galaxy could become a lonely island of stars in a sea of darkness.

Bangs and crunches

Some scientists suggest that the Universe doesn't just have a beginning and an end, but a series of Big Bangs and Big Crunches. We could be living in the first Universe in this cycle... or the millionth.

Astronomy timeline

These pages show when some of the important events in the history of astronomy took place. The earlier dates that don't give an exact year are estimates.

13.7 billion years ago
The Big Bang

12 billion years ago
The first galaxies appear.

5 billion years ago
The Sun is born.

4 billion years ago
The Earth is born.

600,000 years ago
Humans first appear on the earth.

5,000 years ago
Construction of Stonehenge begins.

5,000 years ago
Written astronomical records made in Sumer.

5,000 years ago
Egyptians use astronomy to predict floods.

3,250 years ago
Ancient kingdom of Babylon becomes hotbed of astronomical activity.

2,500 years ago
Greek astronomers make big leaps forward.

A little under 2000 years ago
Ptolemy develops his theories about the Universe.

From about the year 800
Islamic astronomers build on Greek discoveries.

1543
Copernicus's theory that the Earth goes round the Sun is published.

1608
The telescope is invented.

1609
Galileo makes improvements on the telescope.

1633
Galileo is put on trial.

1660s
Isaac Newton discovers gravity.

1675 London's Royal Observatory is founded.

1781 William Herschel discovers Uranus.

1845 William Parsons builds largest telescope to date.

1916 Albert Einstein publishes new theory of gravity.

1920s Edwin Hubble discovers galaxies are moving apart.

1930 Pluto is discovered.

1937 The radio telescope is invented.

1940s Big Bang theory is developed.

1957 *Sputnik 1* is launched into space.

1960s Space Race is in full swing.

1969 The first man on the Moon.

1970 Near-fatal *Apollo 13* mission.

1975 Russian probes land on Venus.

1976 The US *Viking* probes land on Mars.

1981 The first Space Shuttle *Columbia* is launched.

1986 Soviet Union launches space station *Mir*.

1986 Space Shuttle *Challenger* disaster.

1990 The Hubble Space Telescope is launched.

1998 Construction of the International Space Station (ISS) begins.

2003 NASA *Columbia* disaster.

2006 Pluto is demoted from planet to dwarf planet.

2008 *Phoenix* probe finds frozen water on Mars.

2008 The LHC is switched on at CERN.

Today Thousands of satellites orbit the Earth and astronauts are living on the ISS.

2020 Moon base to be built.

Star charts

It can take a lot of time and patience to spot constellations. But it's a lot easier if you use star charts. The charts on the next few pages tell you where all the constellations and stars are at different times of the year, and in different hemispheres.

Northern hemisphere

Looking north

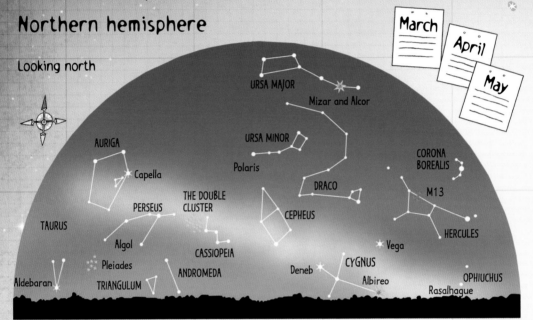

Looking south

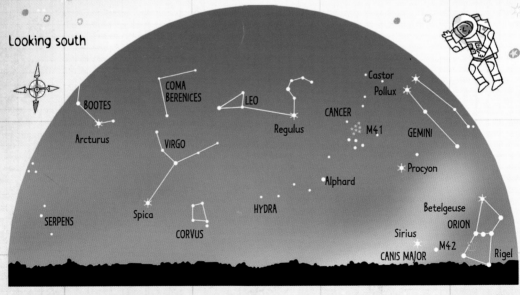

Key: Open cluster (a group of young stars)   Double star (two stars together)   Nebula (a cloud of gas and dust)   Galaxy (a huge group of stars)   Globular cluster (a group of old stars)

One good way to tell stars from planets is that stars twinkle and planets don't. You can see this even when you're looking at them without binoculars or a telescope.

Northern hemisphere

June

July

Aug

Looking north

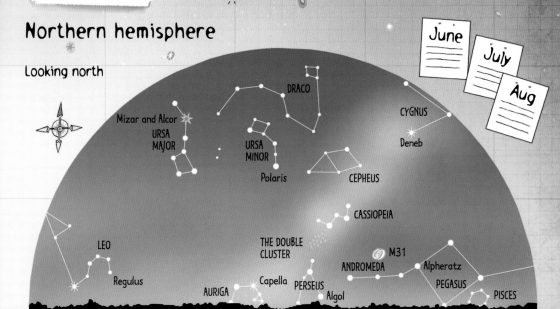

DRACO

Mizar and Alcor
URSA MAJOR

URSA MINOR

Polaris

CYGNUS
Deneb

CEPHEUS

CASSIOPEIA

LEO

Regulus

THE DOUBLE CLUSTER

AURIGA   Capella   PERSEUS   Algol

M31
ANDROMEDA   Alpheratz

PEGASUS

PISCES

Looking south

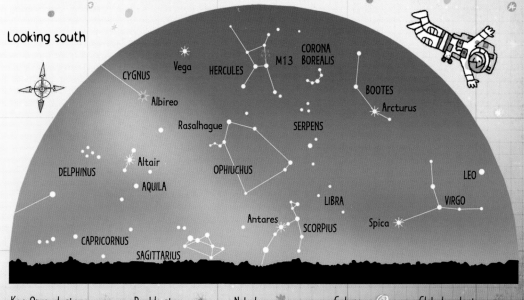

Vega   HERCULES   M13   CORONA BOREALIS

CYGNUS

Albireo

Rasalhague   SERPENS   BOOTES
Arcturus

Altair

DELPHINUS   OPHIUCHUS

AQUILA

LEO

VIRGO

LIBRA   Spica

Antares   SCORPIUS

CAPRICORNUS

SAGITTARIUS

Key: Open cluster
(a group of young stars)

Double star
(two stars together)

Nebula
(a cloud of gas and dust)

Galaxy
(a huge group of stars)

Globular cluster
(a group of old stars)

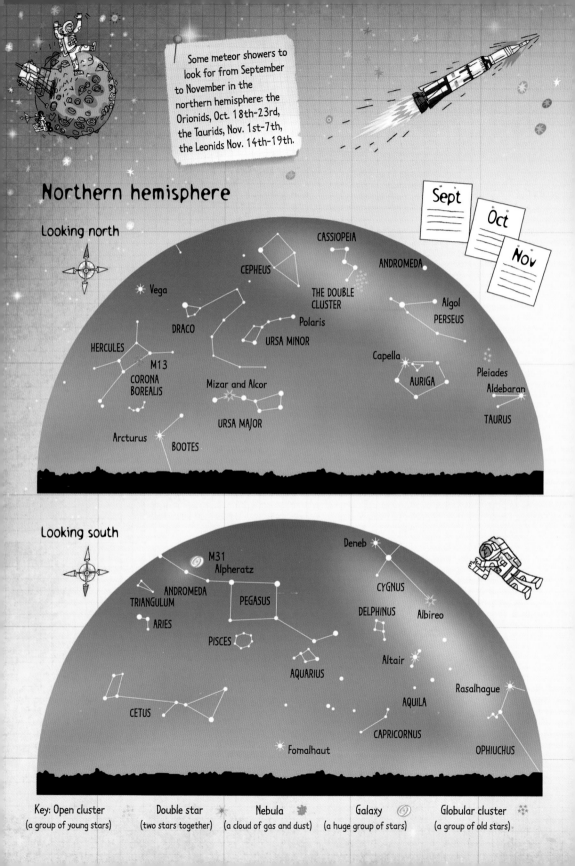

Some meteor showers to look for from September to November in the northern hemisphere: the Orionids, Oct. 18th-23rd, the Taurids, Nov. 1st-7th, the Leonids Nov. 14th-19th.

Northern hemisphere

Looking north

Sept

Oct

Nov

CASSIOPEIA

CEPHEUS

ANDROMEDA

Vega

THE DOUBLE CLUSTER

Algol
PERSEUS

DRACO

Polaris

URSA MINOR

HERCULES

M13
CORONA BOREALIS

Capella

AURIGA

Pleiades
Aldebaran

Mizar and Alcor

URSA MAJOR

TAURUS

Arcturus

BOOTES

Looking south

M31
Alpheratz

Deneb

ANDROMEDA

CYGNUS

TRIANGULUM

PEGASUS

DELPHINUS

Albireo

ARIES

PISCES

AQUARIUS

Altair

CETUS

AQUILA

Rasalhague

CAPRICORNUS

OPHIUCHUS

Fomalhaut

Key: Open cluster
(a group of young stars)

Double star
(two stars together)

Nebula
(a cloud of gas and dust)

Galaxy
(a huge group of stars)

Globular cluster
(a group of old stars)

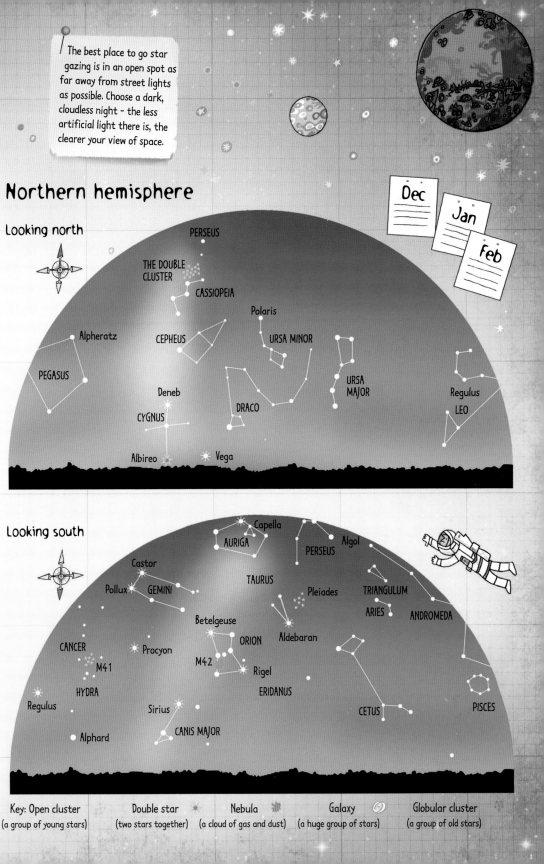

The best place to go star gazing is in an open spot as far away from street lights as possible. Choose a dark, cloudless night – the less artificial light there is, the clearer your view of space.

Dec

Jan

Feb

Northern hemisphere

Looking north

PERSEUS

THE DOUBLE CLUSTER

CASSIOPEIA

Polaris

Alpheratz

CEPHEUS

URSA MINOR

PEGASUS

URSA MAJOR

Deneb

DRACO

Regulus

CYGNUS

LEO

Albireo   Vega

Looking south

Capella

AURIGA

Algol

PERSEUS

Castor

TRIANGULUM

Pollux   GEMINI

TAURUS

Pleiades

ARIES

ANDROMEDA

Betelgeuse

Aldebaran

CANCER

Procyon

ORION

M41

M42

Rigel

HYDRA

ERIDANUS

Regulus

Sirius

CETUS

PISCES

Alphard

CANIS MAJOR

Key: Open cluster
(a group of young stars)   Double star ✳
(two stars together)   Nebula ✺
(a cloud of gas and dust)   Galaxy ◎
(a huge group of stars)   Globular cluster
(a group of old stars)

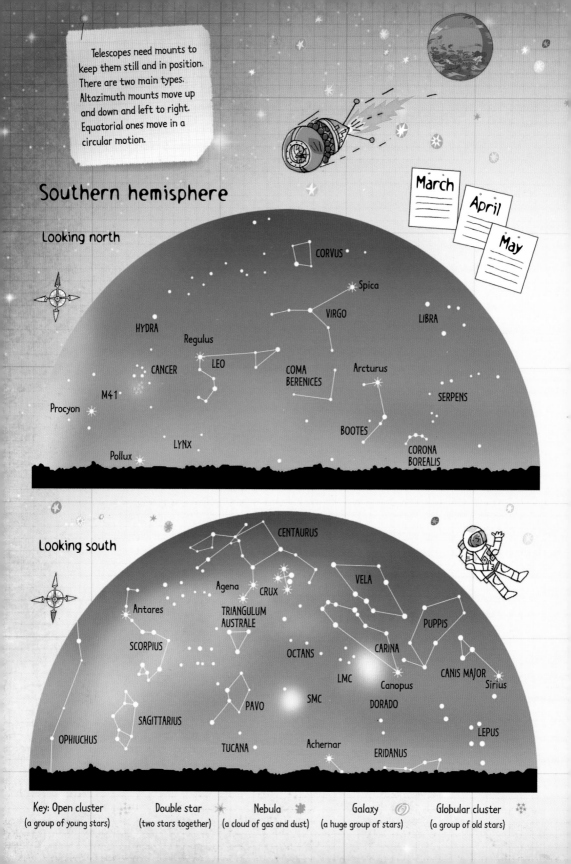

Telescopes need mounts to keep them still and in position. There are two main types. Altazimuth mounts move up and down and left to right. Equatorial ones move in a circular motion.

March

April

May

Southern hemisphere

Looking north

CORVUS

Spica

VIRGO

LIBRA

HYDRA

Regulus

LEO

Arcturus

SERPENS

CANCER

COMA BERENICES

M41

Procyon

BOOTES

CORONA BOREALIS

LYNX

Pollux

Looking south

CENTAURUS

VELA

Agena

CRUX

Antares

TRIANGULUM AUSTRALE

PUPPIS

SCORPIUS

OCTANS

CARINA

CANIS MAJOR

LMC

Canopus

Sirius

SMC

DORADO

PAVO

SAGITTARIUS

TUCANA

Achernar

LEPUS

OPHIUCHUS

ERIDANUS

Key: Open cluster
(a group of young stars)

Double star
(two stars together)

Nebula
(a cloud of gas and dust)

Galaxy
(a huge group of stars)

Globular cluster
(a group of old stars)

If you're using a telescope, start off with an eyepiece with low magnification. You'll be able to see a wide section of the sky, which makes it easier to find things.

Southern hemisphere

June
July
Aug

Looking north

Antares
SCORPIUS
SAGITTARIUS
CAPRICORNUS
LIBRA
OPHIUCHUS
AQUILA
SERPENS
Altair
AQUARIUS
Albireo
HERCULES
DELPHINUS
Spica
CORONA
BOREALIS
M13
Vega
VIRGO
Arcturus
CYGNUS
BOOTES
DRACO
Deneb

Looking south

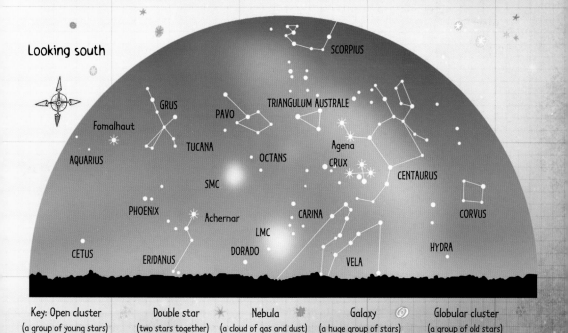

SCORPIUS
GRUS
TRIANGULUM AUSTRALE
PAVO
Fomalhaut
Agena
TUCANA
CRUX
AQUARIUS
OCTANS
CENTAURUS
SMC
PHOENIX
CORVUS
Achernar
CARINA
LMC
CETUS
DORADO
HYDRA
ERIDANUS
VELA

Key: Open cluster
(a group of young stars)　　Double star
(two stars together)　　Nebula
(a cloud of gas and dust)　　Galaxy
(a huge group of stars)　　Globular cluster
(a group of old stars)

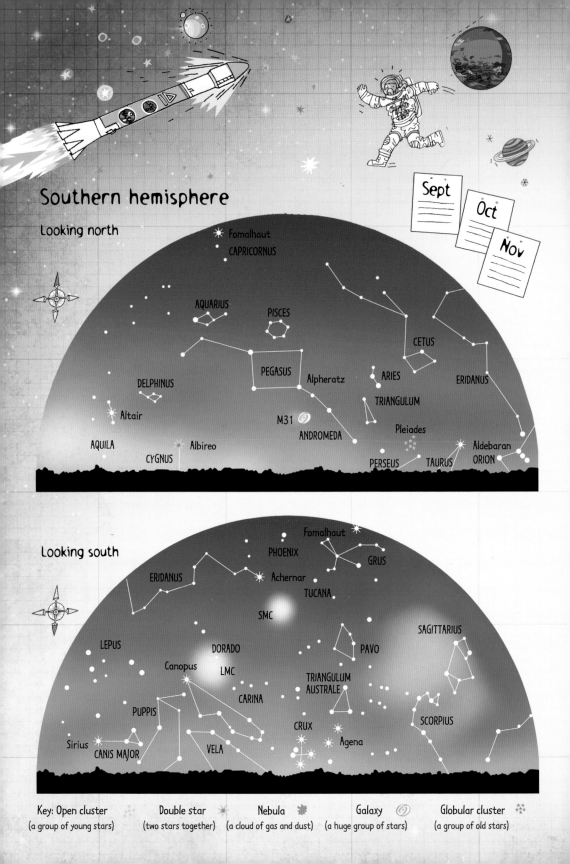

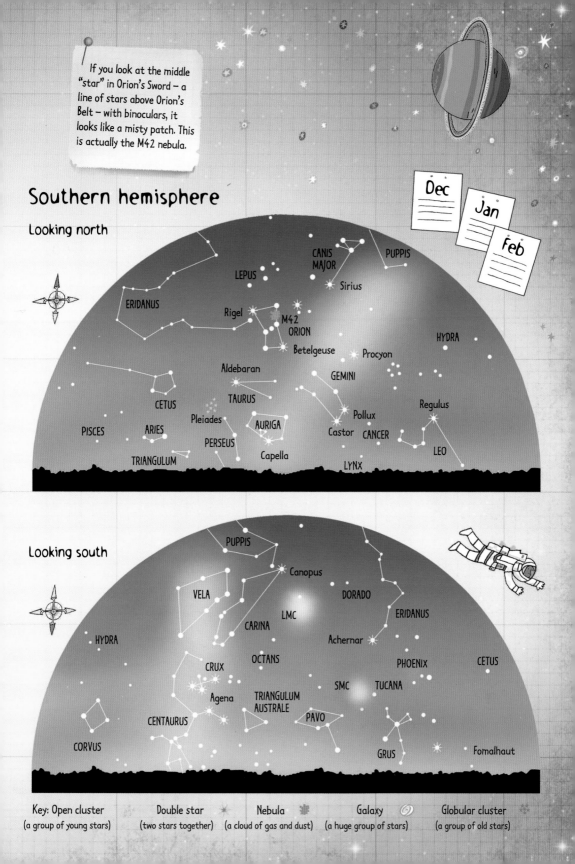

If you look at the middle "star" in Orion's Sword – a line of stars above Orion's Belt – with binoculars, it looks like a misty patch. This is actually the M42 nebula.

Southern hemisphere

Looking north

Dec
Jan
Feb

CANIS MAJOR
PUPPIS
LEPUS
Sirius
ERIDANUS
Rigel
M42
ORION
HYDRA
Betelgeuse
Procyon
Aldebaran
GEMINI
TAURUS
Regulus
CETUS
Pollux
PISCES
ARIES
Pleiades
AURIGA
Castor
CANCER
LEO
PERSEUS
Capella
TRIANGULUM
LYNX

Looking south

PUPPIS
Canopus
VELA
DORADO
LMC
ERIDANUS
CARINA
HYDRA
Achernar
OCTANS
PHOENIX
CETUS
CRUX
SMC
TUCANA
Agena
TRIANGULUM AUSTRALE
CENTAURUS
PAVO
CORVUS
GRUS
Fomalhaut

Key: Open cluster (a group of young stars)   Double star (two stars together)   Nebula (a cloud of gas and dust)   Galaxy (a huge group of stars)   Globular cluster (a group of old stars)

Glossary

In this glossary, you can find explanations for some of the words you'll come across in this book. The words in *italic type* have their own entry elsewhere in the glossary.

ASTEROID A lump of rock or metal (or a mix of both) orbiting the *Sun*.

ASTEROID BELT Area beyond *Mars* where there are lots of *asteroids* and some *dwarf planets*.

ASTROLOGY Group of beliefs according to which the relative positions of *stars* and *planets* are used to predict what will happen to people born at certain times of the year. Someone who does astrology is known as an astrologer.

ASTRONAUT The name for an American or European person who goes into space.

ASTRONOMER A scientist who studies space, *planets*, *stars* and other objects found in space.

ATMOSPHERE The layers of gases surrounding a large object in space, such as a *planet*.

BIG BANG The theory that says the *Universe* had a sudden, violent beginning.

BIG CRUNCH The theory that one day the *Universe* will collapse in on itself.

BLACK HOLE Objects in space that have such a strong gravitational pull that they drag in everything around them. Not even light can escape, which is why they are black.

COMET A bundle of ice, dust and rock that has a gassy "tail" and is in *orbit* around our *Sun* or another sun.

COMPOUND TELESCOPE An *optical telescope* that uses both mirrors and lenses to gather and focus light.

CONSTELLATION A group of *stars* that appears to us to form a pattern in the sky.

COSMONAUT The name for a Russian person who goes into space.

DIAMETER The distance across the middle of a circle or through the middle of a sphere.

DWARF PLANET An object in *orbit* around a star that's too small to be considered a *planet*, but is larger than an *asteroid*.

EARTH Our home *planet*. It's the third planet out from the *Sun*.

ECLIPSE The partial or total disappearance of an object in space when another object passes between it and the viewer. An eclipse of the *Sun* is known as a *solar* eclipse. An eclipse of the *Moon* is a *lunar* eclipse.

EXOPLANET A *planet* orbiting another *star* beyond our *Solar System*.

EXTRA VEHICULAR ACTIVITY (EVA) The technical term for going outside a spacecraft.

EXTRA TERRESTRIAL Life form from somewhere other than *Earth*.

GALAXY A vast collection of *stars*.

GAS GIANT A large *planet* that's mainly made up of gas and liquid, rather than rock. In our *Solar System*, the gas giants are *Jupiter*, *Saturn*, *Uranus* and *Neptune*.

GEOCENTRIC Geocentric theories said that the *Sun* and *planets* *orbit* the *Earth*.

GRAVITY A force that tries to pull two objects together. The more *matter* an object has the stronger its pull.

HELIOCENTRIC Heliocentric theories say that the *Earth* and other *planets* *orbit* the *Sun*.

INNER PLANETS The four rocky *planets*, *Mercury, Venus, Earth* and *Mars*, whose *orbits* are smaller than those of the *gas giants*.

JUPITER The fifth *planet* out from the *Sun*.

KUIPER BELT An area of the *Solar System* beyond the *planets*, containing rocky objects and some *dwarf planets*, including *Pluto*.

LIGHT YEAR The distance that light travels in a year – about 9.5 trillion km or 5.9 trillion miles.

LUNAR To do with our *Moon*.

MARS The fourth *planet* out from the *Sun*.

MASS The amount of *matter* that an object is made of. Weight is calculated as mass times the gravitational pull of wherever you are.

MATTER A scientific word for the stuff that everything in the *Universe* is made of.

MERCURY The closest *planet* to the *Sun*.

METEOR A *meteoroid* that burns up as it reaches the *atmosphere*.

METEORITE A *meteoroid* that has landed on the *Earth*'s surface.

METEOROID A piece of dust or rock in space.

MOON A natural *satellite* that orbits a *planet* or other large object in space. Our Moon is written with a capital M.

NATIONAL AERONAUTICS AND SPACE ADMINISTRATION (NASA) The part of the US government that's responsible for space travel.

NEBULA A swirling cloud of gas and dust where *stars* are born.

NEPTUNE The eighth *planet* out from the *Sun*.

OORT CLOUD A cloud of *comets* that's believed to exist at the edge of the *Solar System*.

OPTICAL TELESCOPE A *telescope* that uses lenses or mirrors to gather and focus light.

ORBIT To circle around another object in space. The route a particular object takes around another is also known as its orbit.

PLANET A large sphere in *orbit* around a *star*, such as the *Sun*.

PLUTO Used to be the ninth *planet* from the *Sun*, now classified as a *plutoid*.

PLUTOID A type of large *dwarf planet*.

RADIO TELESCOPE A type of *telescope* used to detect radio waves – a type of light that we can't see with our own eyes.

RED GIANT A *star* that is running out of fuel and is swelling up as it cools down.

REFLECTOR TELESCOPE A type of *optical telescope* that uses mirrors to gather light.

REFRACTOR TELESCOPE A type of *optical telescope* that uses lenses to gather light.

ROCKET A vehicle that boosts spacecraft into *orbit*. Rockets can also be used as bombs.

SATELLITE An object that is in *orbit* around a *planet*, *star* or another object in space.

SATURN The sixth *planet* out from the *Sun*.

SOLAR To do with our *Sun*.

SOLAR SYSTEM Our *Sun* and the *planets* and other objects that *orbit* around it.

SPACE RACE The rivalry between the former USSR and the USA to be the first to explore space.

SPACESUIT A sealed suit with an air supply that *astronauts* and *cosmonauts* wear in space.

STAR A burning ball of gas in space.

SUN the *star* at the heart of our *Solar System*. But any star with planets circling it is a sun.

SUPERNOVA An exploding *star*. The plural of supernova is supernovae. Some supernovae are visible from Earth.

TELESCOPE A tool used by *astronomers* to study the skies.

TERRAFORMING Altering a *planet* to make it more like *Earth* so that people can live there. For example, altering its *atmosphere*.

UNIVERSE A name for everything that exists and all of space and time.

URANUS The seventh *planet* out from the *Sun*.

VACUUM A place where there's no air or other gases. Space is a vacuum.

VENUS The second *planet* out from the *Sun*.

WHITE DWARF A small, dense *star* that's near the end of its life.

ZERO GRAVITY The feeling of weightlessness that people experience when they travel in space.

Index

Acknowledgements

Every effort has been made to trace and acknowledge ownership of copyright. If any rights have been omitted, the publishers offer to rectify this in any future editions following notification. The publishers are grateful to the following individuals and organizations for their permission to reproduce material on the following pages: (t=top, b=bottom, l=left, r=right)

p1 NASA,ESA and The Hubble Heritage Team (STScI/AURA); **p2-3** NASA, ESA, N. Smith (U. California, Berkeley) et al., and The Hubble Heritage Team (STScI/AURA); **p6-7** © Amana Images inc./Alamy; **p8** (t) © Simon Stirrup/ Alamy; **p11** © Dennis di Cicco/Corbis; **p13** (b) NASA; **p15** (b) NASA, ESA, and the Hubble Heritage Team (STScI/AURA), Acknowledgment: W. Blair (Johns Hopkins University); **p18-19** © Joshua Strang/US Airforce/ ZUMA/Corbis; **p20** (t) Detlev Van Ravenswaay/SPL; **p21** (b) © David Cortner/Galaxy Picture Library; **p24** (b) © Gallo Images/Alamy; **p26** (b) Francesco Reginato/Stone/Getty Images; **p27** (br) Thierry Legault/ Eurelios/SPL; **p29** (t) NASA/ESA/STScI/The Hubble Heritage Team/SPL; **p30** (b) Debra Meloy Elmegreen (Vassar College) et al. & The Hubble Heritage Team (AURA/STScI/NASA); **p31** (t) © Jon Christensen; **p32** NASA/ ESA/STScI/The Hubble Heritage Team/SPL; **p36** (t) NASA/Johns Hopkins University Applied Physics Laboratory/ Carnegie Institution of Washington; **p37** Courtesy NASA/JPL-Caltech; **p39** Apollo 8/NASA; **p40-41** NASA/JPL-Caltech /Cornell/SPL; **p42** NASA/SPL; **p43** NASA/ESA/STScI/J.Clarke, Boston U./SPL; **p44** (t) NASA/ESA/STScI E.Karkoschka, U.Arizona/SPL; **p45** (b) NASA/SPL; **p46** NASA, ESA, H. Weaver (JHU/APL), A. Stern (SwRI), and the HST Pluto Companion Search Team; **p47** © Gordon Garradd/SPL; **p48** © 2008 The British Library, reference 49.e.15, plate VIII; **p48-49** © Seth Joel/Corbis; **p50-51** © Virtalis Limited; **p54** Whipple Museum of the History of Science, University of Cambridge, Wh.5358.4; **p55** (tr) © Werner Forman/Corbis, (br) Royal Astronomical Society/SPL; **p58** (b) © Science Museum/Science & Society; **p59** © Roger Ressmeyer/Corbis; **p60-61** NASA; **p62** (b) NSSDC, NASA; **p63** (b) © RIA Novosti/TopFoto; **p64** (t) Popperfoto/Getty Images; **65** (r) © RIA Novosti/SPL; **p65** (tr) © RIA Novosti/TopFoto; **p66-67** NASA/SPL; **p68-69** STS-114 Crew, ISS Expedition 11 Crew, NASA; **p70-71** NASA; **p73** NASA; **p74** (b) NASA/SPL; **p76-77** © Roger Ressmeyer/Corbis; **p78** (b) NASA; **p79** NASA and The Hubble Heritage Team (STScI/AURA); **p80** (tl) NASA, (b) courtesy NASA/JPL-Caltech; **p82-83** © Richard Wainscoat/Alamy; **p83** (tr) © Photolibrary/Alamy; **p84-85** Detlev Van Ravenswaay/SPL; **p87** (b) Maximilien Brice,CERN.

Edited by Jane Chisholm. Art director: Mary Cartwright. Picture research by Ruth King. Digital design by John Russell. With thanks to Rachel Firth.